Game-Tested
Football Drills

Game-Tested Football Drills

John W. Durham

PARKER PUBLISHING COMPANY, INC.
West Nyack, NY

GV
954.4
.D87

Library of Congress Cataloging in Publication Data

Durham, John W
  Game-tested football drills.

  Includes index.
  1. Football coaching. I. Title.
GV954.4.D87   796.332'07'7   79-27802
ISBN 0-13-346163-7

How This Book
Will Help You

Coaches agree that all consistently successful football teams execute the fundamentals well. It is through drills that the fundamentals of the game are learned. But many drills fail because they do not properly simulate game conditions.

In this book each drill will be presented and explained so you can understand:

1. The design and purpose of the drill.
2. The preparation you should make to insure effective administration of the drill.
3. The scheduling of the drill and how it fits into practice plans for pre-season, weekly game preparation, and changing situations.
4. How the drill is carried out on the practice field.
5. How the drill is evaluated.

But just a conglomeration of coaching situations is not appropriate. This book is organized so you will be able to utilize the organization of drills on the *three* distinct coaching plateaus:

1. The teaching and repetition of various techniques in the most basic one-on-one situation.

3

2. The step up to various group drills, so the player can gain confidence and experience working with the various components of the team.

3. The ultimate step of working in a full team that enables the player to execute the fundamentals with nearly all the distractions that the game itself provides.

Distinct playing situations are emphasized throughout the book. All drills presented have stood the test of time. One example of the development of a game situation drill is the offensive "Breakaway" in Chapter 6. Careful film review had indicated that the author's offensive backs executed well . . . except, they broke few long gains. Then they started using the drill, which pitted a full offensive unit against third string defensive personnel. The objective of the drill was to get the backs maneuvering in the open field. The drill produced results, culminating in many long runs.

The drills in this book are categorized as to offense, defense, and special teams. All particular on-the-field situations are presented so that you will be able to utilize the book as an effective checklist for both pre-season and week-by-week preparation.

This book points out the elements that must be present to achieve good on-the-field performance. The real battle in coaching is to know what is important, then teach it effectively, allowing the superfluous to fall by the wayside. This book is not dedicated to high sounding or grandiose technical systems of play. It is a down-to-earth day-by-day football coaching manual. It will help you eliminate the unnecessary and get down to the business of winning.

John W. Durham

Contents

Game-Tested
Football Drills

ONE

Warming Up and Conditioning the Squad

THE WARM-UP

An effective warm-up serves two purposes. First, it prepares the player to practice at maximum efficiency. Second, it allows the player to participate in full speed practice drills with less chance of injury.

There was a time when coaches began practice by administering a rigorous calisthenics period, including grass drills, push-ups, pull ups, and the like. Tired athletes will *not* learn techniques efficiently; as a result, the present feeling among coaches seems to be that the initial warm-up period should *not* serve the purpose of conditioning the athletes.

The period devoted to the warm-up should meet the following criteria: (1) prepares the athlete to practice, (2) improves his potential for sprinting by teaching form running, (3) increases his flexibility by doing stretching exercises, (4) does not make him tired, and (5) is completed as rapidly as possible. Of the literally thousands of combinations possible for the warm-up, we tailored ours to fit the preceding criteria.

We have divided our beginning procedures into two phases, consisting of form running and stretching.

FORM RUNNING

Speed is an element that is of utmost importance to a good football team. Great team speed will make up for many other deficiencies and is often the difference between a mediocre squad and an outstanding squad. A slow defensive team will have many *home runs* scored against it. Just as good coaching can improve any athletic skill, an athlete can increase his speed by bettering his running form. If the practice area is a great distance from the dressing room (300 yards or more), the drill may be accomplished by stationing coaches along the way and having the players proceed to the field by running single file. If the field is closer, the players report to their individual coaches at the intersection of a boundary and a yard line. The players run single file across the field, taking an adjacent line on the way back. Each coach checks the players in his group for good running form.

The toes should be pointed straight ahead while running. If the player places each foot on the ground just outside the marked line and does not cross over, this will insure that the feet are placed correctly and that the toes are pointed. It is remarkable how many athletes do not run a straight line distance from one point to another. This running fault can be attributed to improper toe point and foot placement. By correcting of this fundamental fault, the player can improve his running form significantly.

In form running the player should assume a slight forward body lean that contributes to forward momentum. Too much forward lean causes the individual to be off balance and no lean retards good sprinting form. We are not too picky about correcting this; the player can experiment and attain the correct angular position with some experience.

The runner should land on the ball of each foot, with the heels slightly off the ground. Being up on the toes causes too much strain on the foot, while landing flat on the soles tends to develop a runner with no forward body lean.

Proper arm action is emphasized. The arms should be carried so that the elbows are fairly close to the body with the hands about belt high, moving in planes perpendicular to the ground. The common problem with the arms in running is that they tend to cross in front of the body, which contributes to a distortion in the straight ahead motion of the runner. We stress telling the runner to reach out in front and grab the air, and keep the elbows tight.

Relaxation of the body is imperative in running. Facial, neck, and shoulder muscles must be relaxed or they will cause the rest of the musculature to be taut, which will restrict movement. It is necessary for the coach to carefully observe the runner to insure that he is relaxed throughout the run and that the head is not allowed to flop around or to be held to one side of the body.

Each player runs at half speed, picking up the pace slightly as the drill progresses. Form running must be well supervised, because improvement will not be realized if the players are permitted to do it in a sloppy or careless manner.

Form running elevates the pulse rate of athletes, preparing them for the stretching phase.

STRETCHING

A significant development in modern football is the interest in flexibility that has been exhibited on all levels of play. Some professional teams have employed flexibility coaches to direct the stretching program. We do not feel that we can devote as much time to flexibility as many authorities recommend because of all the other things that must be accomplished in the limited time on the practice field. Consequently, we have developed an abbreviated routine that can be accomplished in about four minutes. Other "flex" exercises can be incorporated in the locker room prior to taking the field, particularly the carrying out of individual routines, as each athlete's needs are different in terms of which specific muscular limitations must be overcome. This is of obvious importance in the area of rehabilitation.

The exercises that we prescribe for the practice field serve the purposes of increasing the flow of blood to the muscles, preparing them for a vigorous and sustained series of efforts. A secondary and long-term benefit of the flexibility exercises is to gradually increase the athlete's general flexibility as the season progresses. The exercises are directed by the coaches within the various individual groups (i.e., defensive ends with defensive end coach, etc.). The exercises are:

1. Groin stretch—The player puts the lead foot flat on the ground, the back foot as far back as possible, with the chest just over the knee of the lead leg. The toes should be pointed in the direction of the lean. As in all flexibility exercises, the stretch should increase gradually so the tissue will not be damaged by sudden ballistic movements. After about twenty seconds in the initial direction, the player adjusts his feet to approximately shoulder width, knees at a fairly straight attitude but not locked, then bends down at the hips, attempting to touch the ground with the elbows. Once again bouncing is discouraged, since the objective is to gradually increase the flexibility of the musculature. After about ten seconds in the middle, the player stretches in the opposite direction, then come to the middle again. Next, he leans to the right but points the toes perpendicular to the direction of the lean. When he again returns to the middle, he will attempt to touch the ground behind his legs by reaching as far as he can. The athlete who can increase his groin flexibility should be able to increase his natural stride length, which will increase his speed.

2. Back and hamstring stretch—The player puts his hands on his hips, feet about shoulder width apart, and leans back as far as he can, approximating a limbo position. Then he locks his knees, and bends down with the hips, attempting to touch the ground. His goal is to touch with the palms of his hands, but he must not allow his knees to unlock. Twenty repetitions are done. Last, he will bring the feet closer together, bend over and grab the toe cleats with the hands, then slowly rotate the knees as far back as he can. He does this twice.

3. Quadriceps stretch—The player kneels on the ground and attempts to lie down and place the back of his shoulders on the ground; failing that, he will go as far back as he is able. He does this twice.

4. Trunk rotation—Although this is not a true flex exercise, it does serve the purpose of "loosening up" the middle torso. With a good bend at the waist, the player rotates his upper torso counterclockwise, reversing to clockwise, then revers-

ing a third and fourth time. Fifteen seconds is sufficient for the exercise.

5. Neck rotation—Again this is a general loosening exercise in which the athlete rotates his neck by using the point of his chin as a point on a circle. Three reverses and fifteen seconds will accomplish the exercise.

6. Arm rotation—The player loosens the shoulder girdle by making large circles with the hands describing the movement of a clock with the face perpendicular to the ground. A few reverses are called for. A second phase of the exercise has the athlete make small circles with the hands extended directly out from the sides.

7. Jumps—This is a warm-up that is designed to get the players to do something explosive with their legs, preparing them for full-speed starts and agility drills. The players jump twenty times. The first set of ten jumps are progressive, that is, each jump should be higher than the previous one, building up to a maximum on the tenth jump. In the second set, the athlete makes ten maximum jumps. The exercise is performed by taking off from both feet, using the arms to aid in the maximum effort.

All form running and general warm-up exercises are done before every practice throughout the season with the following exceptions: (1) they are not done before the short practices (held on three separate days) in the middle of the day in the pre-season, (2) they are not done on the day prior to the game, and (3) they are eliminated on the day following the game. Otherwise, the only adjustment is that ten maximum repetitions of the jump are made rather than the twenty called for during the pre-season. The routine is standard and each coach can teach it to his players when the season begins. After it becomes habit, the players can proceed through the progression rapidly, but the coach must supervise so that the work is properly done.

ENDING PRACTICE

Wind sprints and conditioning bouts at the end of practice have been used by coaches since the days of Stagg. There are two widely divergent points of view in regard to the use of post practice conditioning drills. One extreme viewpoint insists on loading up the player with lots of conditioning work, possibly running twenty or twenty-five 40-yard dashes or an equally demanding regimen. The arguments for such a routine are good. The player will obviously be in good physical condition, a necessity for consistently good performance and a safeguard against injury. A tough conditioning routine can build spirit among the players and generally improve team morale. At the opposite pole, some coaches theorize that no conditioning work should be done at the end of practice, advancing arguments that are also sound and logical. The players may tend to "go all out" and not pace themselves if they are aware that there will be no "extra" work at the end of the regular practice, making for better concentration during the learning phase of practice.

My own approach to winding up practice has undergone an evolution from a stiff and demanding schedule of exercises to the present method in which a very brief workout is done at the end of the regular practice. With that in mind, all of practice is structured so that nearly the entire session is of high intensity. The objective is to accomplish what needs to be done as efficiently as possible, so that most of the conditioning occurs incidentally. If conditioning drills are minimized, much of the sheer drudgery connected with them disappears, enabling the player to better concentrate during practice. We either do starts or 40-yeard dashes when we do some conditioning work at the end of practice.

STARTS

The most important fundamental in offensive football is the execution of the offensive snap. Starts are scheduled at the end of the offensive practices in the pre-season (evenings) and every Monday (game day Friday) during the playing season. The team is broken down so that there are as many offensive lines as are available, lined up on a yard stripe. The first line works with the first quarterback, the second unit with the second quarterback, and so on. The coach places a ball on the ground near, but not on a yard stripe, signaling the first unit to run up and align on the ball. The quarterback gives a snap count, sets the line, and calls the signals. The ball is snapped and the line and quarterback take a 10-yard dash, slowing up and floating the following ten yards. The ball is flipped to a coach or manager and the team aligns on another ball and carries out another start. The second unit and the third unit follow behind. Additional personnel line up with the third unit on the line of scrimmage. Coaches must check splits, alignments, and starts. This is a discipline drill, as the players are tired and they must execute the starting count correctly or they simply repeat the drill. If your squad falters in the late stages of a game or jumps offside near the goal line, think about this drill. Concentration is an absolute must!

The backs other than the quarterbacks are in another group for their starts. At one time we had the entire team run perfect plays, but we felt this took a bit too much time. The backfield coach aligns the backs and gives them starts in groups just as the line coaches do with their groups. We run ten to twelve perfect starts. During game weeks, from time to time we may tack on two or three 40-yard dashes in addition to the starts.

FORTIES

The 40-yard dash is a widely accepted reference for speed in football. Players are clocked for a distance of forty yards and are evaluated as prospects by professional and college teams partially on the basis of 40-yard dash speed. The kicking game, long passes, and long runs usually come out to be a series of dashes about forty yards in length.

After the morning practices (defensive practice) during the pre-season and after Tuesday practice (Friday game day) during the season, we run forties. The players are broken into defensive groups and each coach ordinarily further divides his unit into two more groups. Each group is given a starting count and dashes at top speed for forty yards. We do from five to eight of these dashes. They provide a good finish for practice and improve stamina. When game day is Friday, we do no forties or starts after practice on Wednesdays or Thursdays.

WARM DOWNS

Cooper and other exercise physiologists agree that it is best to end vigorous physical activity with mild exercise in order to "cool off" an engine that has been laboring at top speed. At one time, we emphasized some light stretching at the end of practice, but now we simply have the players slowly jog into the locker room. Where the field is adjacent to the dressing area, it may be advisable to have the players run a slow lap around the practice field; an even better alternative is to have the players undergo 300 yards of form running just as in the beginning of practice.

IN SEASON WEIGHT TRAINING

Darden, Jones, and others emphasize that the strength levels of football players will drop off as the season progresses unless they are actively participating in a good strength-training routine. Consequently, a growing trend among football coaches is to conduct strength programs during the actual competitive season. The requirements of such a program are that it not be too time consuming and that it not unduly fatigue the athletes.

We have developed a system in which the athletes lift every other day in pre-season workouts and once each week during the season, necessitating four groups for the first schedule and three groups for the second. Pre-season workouts are followed by a group in the weight room both mornings and evenings; in season when there is a Friday game, a group is in the weight room following Monday, Tuesday, and Wednesday practices.

Weight lifting equipment can range from free weights to the most expensive variable resistance machinery on the market. Our program has been geared to a tubular steel frame device in which the resistances are locked with a pin. The routine consists of squats, leg extensions, leg presses, leg curls, bench presses, lat pulldowns, side lateral raises, shoulder presses, arm curls, reverse arm curls, and neck exercises. All exercises are to be done slowly and in good form, accentuating control of the resistance throughout the entire range of motion. One set of all the exercises is accomplished. The aim is to accomplish ten repetitions of each exercise. If the athlete can accomplish ten repetitions, he will add ten pounds to the resistance and do as many reps as possible. When he has again progressed to ten repetitions in good form, he once more adds another ten pounds resistance. The neck exercises and the side lateral raises are accomplished without weights by using a partner to provide resistance while the player is carrying out the exercise. The partner provides enough resistance so that the subject will be unable to do more than ten repetitions. To accomplish side lateral raises, the player has his partner hold his wrists from behind him while his arms are down at his sides. He raises his arms sideways with the elbows fairly straight. The partner will resist the player both coming up and going down. This is not an isometric exercise. The neck exercises are done front, both sides, and back by resisting the individual's movement in all four directions.

THE FITNESS TEST

Prior to the opening of pre-season drills, we administer a fitness test. We believe that it gives us a qunatitative reading on the cardiovascular fitness, strength levels, and sprint speed of all our players. In the fitness test, we have the players make a 1½ mile run, test them for three repetitions maximum on bench and shoulder press and six repetitions maximum on leg press. Each player is timed twice in the 40-yard dash.

The candidates are divided by class, with a county fair system used. While a group is in the weight room, another is running forties, and another is taking the 1½ mile run. In the weight room, each player is to warm up at a very light weight with six to eight repetitions of the exercise. He then is allowed to lift with good form for the three exercises. For uniformity and fairness, the same coach supervises at each weight station throughout the entire test. Managers record results.

For the sprints, players are encouraged to warm up by taking several starts, and are then clocked for forty yards. Each athlete is timed twice, the second time taken by a different coach, with the procedure set up so the same two coaches time all players. The two timers work simultaneously while a coach is at the starting line to insure that the players' fingers are on the line. The watch is started when the runner's hands lift off the ground. Avoid using coaches with "quick" timing hands in order to get reliable results. Records are kept by managers and can be used in the selection of personnel by the coaching staff, particularly in picking specialty teams.

The groups for the 1½ mile run are further broken down into backs and linemen to equalize competition and to cut the number of players on the track at one time. A quarter-mile track is ideal for this purpose. It is advisable to run this in the morning, but whenever it is run, be especially alert for any signs of heat prostration in the players, particularly those who are overweight. We have used a target of twelve minutes as a guide for reasonably good physical condition. We would prefer all players to finish the six laps in less than ten minutes, thirty seconds. We do not disqualify anyone from practicing if the 1½ mile time is poor, but the players who cannot finish in fourteen minutes are in very poor physical condition and must be carefully observed in practice sessions for signs of exhaustion. If the players are aware in the early spring that they will be tested for the 1½ mile run, most will make a conscientious effort to achieve a reasonable level of cardiovascular fitness in the summer months.

The fitness test encourages the players to prepare themselves to do well, as they want to make a good showing for the coaches and their fellow players. The results of the test serve as a valuable guide for the coaches, although ultimate decisions on personnel placement are based on field performance.

TWO

Developing an Offensive Line Through Individual Game-Tested Drills

Have you had offensive linemen who lacked quickness? Were small? Were not aggressive? I have coached offensive linemen lacking in one or two of the preceding categories, yet many of them played regularly and did an adequate job. As a group, offensive linemen are generally the worst athletes in football. Nevertheless, the consistently successful offensive teams control the line of scrimmage because coaching "takes" more with this group than with any other. Some coaches are enamored with the latest "fads" or the tactical phase of the game, neglecting the bedrock, offensive line play. Good offensive line coaches pay attention to detail, but do not overburden the players with too many verbal instructions or do's and don'ts.

Analyze your offensive and (1) decide what the line *must* accomplish in order to make the offense go, (2) determine how the players will execute the necessary fundamentals of the offense, and (3) decide how to coach the players to execute the fundamentals, since the biggest choices in coaching are what *not* to coach rather than what to coach.

STANCE

Study your game films carefully. I have found that a poor stance will cause a poor start, which will cause a poor block. It is inevitable that a poor stance will lead to an ineffective block. Stance should be emphasized in every blocking drill, so we use the stance drill itself as an initial teaching drill and as a review drill for the first few days of practice, then discontinue the drill, since we check the stance in all other offensive line drills. I can not underestimate the importance of effectively coaching the stance, however.

We literally want to knock the defense off the ball as far as we can at the point of attack, preventing penetration on the backside, and walling off or running past the defense that is outside the point of attack. If such a concept is successfully employed, the ball carrier will break through a seam in the defensive "bubble" (Diagram 2-1).

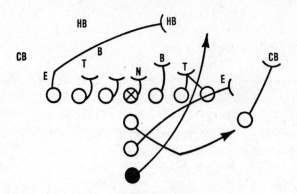

Diagram 2-1
Finding the Seam

Offensive linemen must come off the ball quickly, at an oblique angle in either direction, down the line at a ninety degree angle in either direction, pull down the line, lead or trap in either direction, and execute the pass protection block.

Because of these requirements, we have designed a stance in which the feet are no further apart than shoulder width—a wider stance does not allow the athlete to step laterally with the lead foot. The stance requires the feet to be parallel. A foot stagger would improve the player's ability to step down the line on the side of the back foot but retard his ability to step laterally on the side of the up foot. We coach the offensive linemen to put both hands on the ground. Some coaches believe that the four-point stance hinders mobility and the ability to set for pass protection, but we have found it to make little, if any, difference when compared with the three-point stance. The four-point stance squares up the shoulders and balances the parallel feet nicely. The fingers of the lineman are on the ground, since reaction tests demonstrate that it makes for a quicker take-off than putting the knuckles down. Not much weight is forward on the hands since that would make it difficult to gain ground with a lateral step. The neck is bulled and the back is flat. The heel cleats are just slightly off the ground, which insures that not too much weight is forward.

In coaching the stance, the group is aligned in a three-by-three personnel square (this is adjusted if more or less personnel are available) and each player is instructed to spread his feet the proper width, then to drop his hands in front. The heels are checked to make sure of weight distribution. We also check that the knees are pretty much aligned with the toes.

We spend quite a bit of time coaching the stance on the first day of practice. It is reviewed on the second day, and then the drill is dropped for the rest of the season. After the second day, it is up to the coach to check the stance in all the offensive drills. Ideally, the players learn the stance on the lower levels of play and in the summer conditioning program.

Early in my coaching, I did not get good blocking from my center because I did not emphasize the stance and the amount of weight to place on the ball. In short, I was not detailed enough in my approach to T-formation center play. The T-formation center should be as good a blocker as any other offensive lineman; mine was not. In contrast to my previous approach, I cut down on the width of the center's stance so that it was no wider than shoulder width. When he used the wider spread, he could not snap the ball and step simultaneously. We instruct the center to put both hands on the ball but practically no weight. Previously, with a lot of weight on the ball, he could move forward quickly, but not laterally.

STARTS

For many years I searched for the magic word or the "secret" approach for getting the offensive team off the ball. All the searching taught me was that I had overcomplicated the teaching procedure, overburdening the players with too many fine points. I analyzed what I thought was imperative in the starts, emphasized a couple of points, and we began to achieve better starts.

We like to organize our coaches so that in the pre-season we have one coach for centers, one for guards, one for tackles, and one for ends. You can do this with fewer coaches.

In drilling starts, we place four blocking shields on the ground and take flights of three players to carry out the individual starting drills. In the first segment, the coach aligns the players and instructs them to take three starts with the right foot first. Each flight executes the starting count and drives through the gaps in the shields (Diagram 2-2).

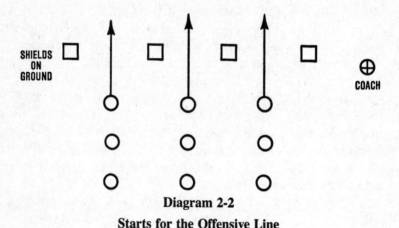

Diagram 2-2

Starts for the Offensive Line

The linemen are coached to mentally shift all the weight to the push off foot (opposite the starting foot) before starting. They will drive off the push-off foot when they hear the starting sound of a non-rhythmic count. It is imperative to come out of the stances level, pumping the arms to propel the body forward.

The second phase of the starting drill has the linemen drive straight through the shields but stepping with the opposite foot first. This is completed in three repetitions.

Next, the players align directly behind the shields and start by stepping off, right foot first, at a forty-five degree angle, through the gap on the right. It is important to come out level, step with the proper foot, and gain distance with the first step (Diagram 2-3). This is followed by three trips at a forty-five degree angle with the left foot first and going to the left. Each of the three flights would align behind the three shields to the right in order to execute the drill to the left side.

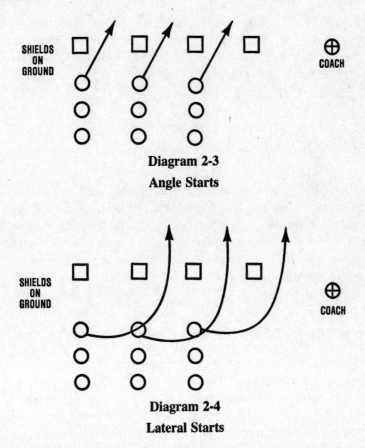

Diagram 2-3

Angle Starts

Diagram 2-4

Lateral Starts

Next the players will align on the shields and step at a ninety degree angle to the line with the right foot first, running down the line to the right, then turning upfield and clearing the next shield (Diagram 2-4). This is followed by two more repetitions, then three lateral starts in the opposite direction. The coach must check for stepping with the proper foot (first step with the foot on the side to which the player is going), as this is the most difficult start we have. A positive step is essential; many players have a tendency to make a very short step or only a pivot on the lead foot. It is required that the players come off level and turn upfield hard after the second step.

Starts are done before every offensive practice in the pre-season, and on Monday and Wednesday during game weeks when the game is on Friday. They are done with the entire line working together on pre-game day and during the warm-up on game day. They must be carefully coached *every single time*! Linemen should never be allowed to execute the starting count poorly. The coaching in the starting drills can be done on the move and the drill can be accomplished at a faster rate as the season progresses, since the players are improving their physical condition. Regardless of the tempo at which the drill is run, it is just as carefully executed at the end of the season as it is at the beginning.

FIT

I did not have success in drawing pictures, explaining, or demonstrating to the players what I mean by "making proper contact." We have a measure of success in teaching the contact phase of the block by using the fit drill. It is used for the first three days of pre-season drills. Its purpose is to give the blockers an excellent mental picture of how contact is to be made for the various blocks. The blocker is walked up to a defender and placed in a proper blocking position on the target. If we are simulating a lineman to be blocked, we have the defender in a low crouched position while the blocker has his shoulder against the hip of the defender and his tail well underneath him. The coach blows a whistle and the blocker accelerates to keep the defender back. We do not subscribe to the wide base and short, choppy step approach. Initial steps in running are naturally short power steps, so it is unnecessary to instruct the players to take short steps. We merely instruct the blocker to run his feet hard and keep his center of gravity underneath him. We do not tell him what to do with his arms, except not to hold his opponent. Many of our blockers will pump their arms in the drive block, since it helps them in running. If the blocker establishes his stance and follows through the way we want him to, everything else will take care of itself.

If a defender is upright we tell the blocker to make his fit at the armpit and accelerate through. The shields are held higher in this drill. In the fit drill, two attempts are made on each hip and two on each armpit.

SIX-POINT HIT OUT

If you check the good game blocks, you will ascertain that the blocker is uncoiling his body at the instant of contact and thrusting through the target. The six-point hit out is done every time individual starts are covered. One group holds the shields at ankle height, while the hit out group extends from six points on a verbal command, extending the eyes through the outside edge of the shield, then recoiling. Each player springs out six times to each shield edge.

DRIVE BLOCK

The greatest reason for breakdowns in the offensive line is that the blocker's footwork is not sustained. After an initial thrust, he overextends his body and goes to the ground. The defender is knocked back a step, recovers, and makes the play. My problem in the coaching of the drive block was that I emphasized the hit out so much that the blocker had no control of his body and, subsequently, could not sustain his foot action. When we took emphasis away from the hit out, and merely emphasized running through the target, we achieved much better success. We never mention uncoiling into the target. If the blocker makes contact and keeps his feet moving against shields in preliminary learning situations, he will eventually learn to uncoil his body while maintaining control of it. He does not need to be told to do this; the progression will usually take place naturally. The six-point hit out will aid the uncoil and give the blocker the idea of how to unload at contact.

The drive block is the basis of all the blocks we coach. In the individual period, we cover the drive block by aligning in a configuration with three players holding blocking shields, and three aligning in stances facing the shields. The blockers are given the snap count and the first block executed is the drive block against a down lineman, who is simulated by the defender holding the shield about knee height. The drive block will be executed by running through the hip of the defender. Three repetitions are carried out to each hip by each group. After finishing the block, the group assumes the shield holders' jobs and the shield holders align behind the new action group.

In the following phase, the shield holders are moved back off the ball to stimulate linebackers. The target is now the armpit, and the blockers run through that point three times on each side.

Variations in the linebacker scheme are then installed by the coach. He instructs the backers to move in the direction of the play on the snap, which will necessitate the blockers giving them a lead. This is done twice in both directions. Finally, the linebackers are asked to blitz directly over the blocker twice.

Defensive linemen are again simulated and are offset slightly in the direction of the play so the blockers are forced to overblock (Diagram 2-5).

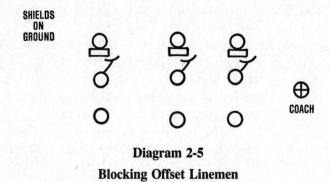

Diagram 2-5
Blocking Offset Linemen

The linemen are then placed in gaps and the blockers are to block them to the inside while the play is aimed in the opposite direction. The target is now the far hip of the lineman and the initial step must be with the near foot driving hard down the line. The blocker must get to the far hip in order to insure that penetration is cut off. The shield holders are to penetrate the gap hard. This is done twice to each side.

It is imperative for a blocking lineman to know his target, step off on the count with the proper foot, and run through the target in every case. Linemen who can not do these things consistently cannot succeed. The drive block drills are covered at the beginning of every offensive practice in the pre-season and on Mondays and Wednesdays for Friday game weeks. We occasionally repeat parts of the drive block drills by using live action by the defenders.

TRAPS

You can trap successfully if the trapper runs the proper route. The process used in pulling for traps is the basis for teaching pulling and leading, cross-blocks, and the like. We do not teach the trap block in the individual period until the day before we introduce the trap plays in the pre-season. The trap drill is repeated on the day the trap plays are installed, the day after, then every other day during the pre-season. In season, we seldom use the drill in the individual period because of the exigencies of time. We believe it is usually sufficient to do our trapping in group and dummy scrimmage periods. If you run an offense that lives or dies with the trap, you should run the drill in the individual period every time you practice offense.

For traps and cross blocks, it is necessary to assume that the target be behind the actual position of the opponent who is to be blocked (Diagram 2-6), which will give the lineman an inside-out

Diagram 2-6
Trap Approach

approach to the defender. This is because the most difficult trap block is one in which the defender does not penetrate but closes to the inside (Diagram 2-7). If there is any penetration by the defender, an adjustment can be made by the blocker without great difficulty, or in many cases the defender has taken himself deep enough to make it impossible to react to the play in time (Diagram 2-8).

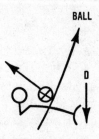

Diagram 2-7

Trapping Closing Defender

Diagram 2-8

Trapping Penetrating Defender

In coaching the linemen to pull, the players are initially aligned in a square configuration and all linemen except the center are taught the hitch step. The entire group will carry out the hitch at the same time by taking the lead foot and moving it so that the toe points in the desired direction of progress. It helps to drive the onside elbow to assist in making the hitch step. The hitch step is taught and reviewed as a separate movement only in the first two trap drills. We think that using it more than that might tend to divorce it from the running part of the trap block, preventing us from putting the elements together as smoothly as we want to.

The next phase of the trap drill is to have two linemen simultaneously pull and run through a gap of shields (Diagram 2-9). This is done twice in each direction. This drill is eliminated after one week in the interests of putting the entire trap action together.

Every time the trap block is drilled in the individual period, shield holders are assigned, and the blockers pull and make the traps in pairs (Diagram 2-10), two reps to each side. Occasionally this drill is done live.

A drill that is used about twice during the pre-season and infrequently during the regular season involves the trapper pulling and three defenders holding shields with a knee on the ground. On the pull the coach will call a name, and the one called will rise, causing the trapper to adjust his path and execute the trap (Diagram 2-11).

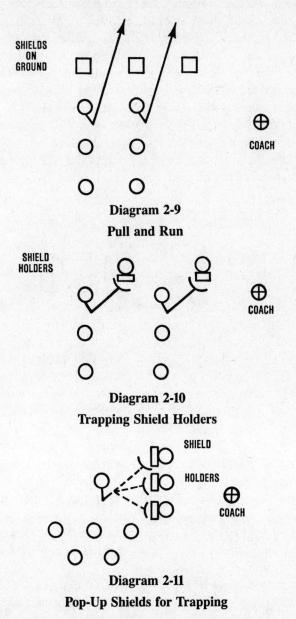

Diagram 2-9

Pull and Run

Diagram 2-10

Trapping Shield Holders

Diagram 2-11

Pop-Up Shields for Trapping

LEADS

Observe young linemen who are leading the play. The big problem is turning the body upfield in order to run a proper route. The tendency is to run a long turning radius, unnecessarily stringing the play to the sideline. Since leads result from an initial pulling movement, the hitch step coaching procedure need not be repeated. The first portion of the lead drill has the players align, hitch, and run parallel to the line, leading through a hole formed by two shields. The turn upfield is executed by turning the head and eyes to the inside and dropping the inside shoulder (Diagram 2-12). The pull and lead drill is executed twice to each side. We do the drill on the day the first play involving a lead is taught and on two subsequent days. We feel it is no longer necessary after the initial periods, since we wish to combine the hitch, run, and block.

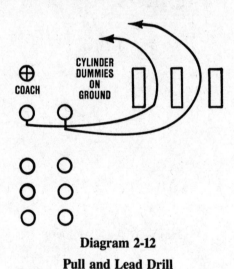

Diagram 2-12

Pull and Lead Drill

We follow the lead and run by combining it with a shield block. The lead and block is done the first two days and repeated on alternate days during the pre-season as part of the individual period (Diagram 2-13). The drill is done twice to each side. We do not do the drill in the regular season since we believe that we get enough pull and lead action in group and team work. The lead block is characterized by the blocker running a predesigned path and blocking out or trapping any penetrating defender; seeing none, he

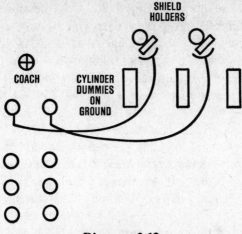

Diagram 2-13

Pull, Lead, and Block Drill

will turn upfield and lead, as indicated in the last progression of the pull drill. The blocker will take the shield holder according to which path he chooses. We do the drill twice to each side (Diagram 2-14).

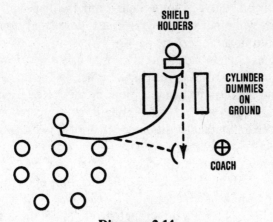

Diagram 2-14

Pulling and Leading or Kicking Out

PASSIVE PASS BLOCK

Our limitations in pass blocking stemmed from overextension. It seemed as though the good defenders were neutralized, then recovered before our blockers could, thus pressuring the passer. What worked for us was to place nearly all the emphasis on *position* and then to coach the use of the hands and arms as almost a second thought. We found it to be much more effective.

We have the linemen initially line up with six or seven yards between them, each man facing a defender, then the defenders take off, with the blockers moving the feet and merely positioning themselves properly in front of the defenders. The blocker wants to align the long axis of his body between the defender and the passer he is protecting. He strives to keep the defender nose up; to allow him on his hip is the first step in being defeated. The defenders will stop themselves and avoid contact in the drill; it is simply a position drill.

We expand the mirror drill that is used in the early days of practice and then include contact in the drill. The defender will not make an all out rush, but will draw one "shock" from the blocker, then attempt to redirect his charge. The blocker will position properly, and drive fists into the sternum of the rusher when he has closed the protector. He is coached to uncoil only with the arms. When we emphasized that, we found that the player would, in time, learn to uncoil and get some help from the legs but would not overextend, while if we emphasized uncoiling from the thighs, the player would invariably overextend.

The next step in the progression is to have the defender attempt to make an all out rush on the passer. When the defender closes the blocker and the blocker is in position, the offensive lineman strikes out at the defender's chest, attempting to gain separation. He must maintain separation and position; those are the two requirements to be an effective pass blocker.

We must prepare the blocker to adjust his block when he does lose position. We align the defenders on the hips of the blockers and on the whistle have them accelerate to the passer. The blocker drives for a down block by running through the far hip of the defender who has him beaten.

We progress to a full speed rendition of the drill by having our best defenders go against the best blockers and attempt to put some genuine pass rush moves on the blocker. An element of competition is involved if a hat represents the passer and the coach picks up the hat three seconds after the play begins. If the defender gets to the hat before that time, he picks up the hat. It is a good idea to keep track of the "pick-ups" and select a winner for the drill.

It may be advantageous for footwork to have two defenders aligned so that the blocker positions and strikes the first defender who halts his charge, then repositions for the second defender who has immediately initiated his charge. The blocker can shuffle and strike five of six times this way. We do not use a steady diet of the drill, but we have helped pass blockers improve footwork by its use.

RECEIVER DRILLS

The ends participate in receiver drills. This is another phase of the game in which the athletes and the coaches can easily see the improvement on a day-to-day basis. The elements essential for developing better receivers are (1) concentration on the ball throughout all receiver drills and during all passing drills, (2) the opportunity to catch many passes from positions simulating positions the receiver would find himself in during game play, and (3) good drill organization so that many balls can be caught in a short period of time. There should be plenty of footballs for the drill and it is good to work against a net so the retrieval of the balls is simplified. A tremendous amount of work can be accomplished in a short period to time in utilizing the receiver drills efficiently.

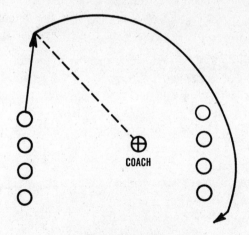

Diagram 2-15
Lob Passes—Alternate Lines

First, the coach or manager lobs short easy passes to the ends as they run under control in order to keep eyes on the ball to make the easy catch (Diagram 2-15). The fundamentals of receiving are to watch the ball all the way to possession, to catch with the little fingers together unless the ball is delivered in front and above the waist (which means thumbs together), and to put it away.

The receivers will make about six catches each (three from each side), then will repeat the process by making one-hand catches.

In the next segment of the drill, the receivers will run crossfield in front of a net and make a reception while crossing. The ball is thrown a bit harder for this phase (Diagram 2-16).

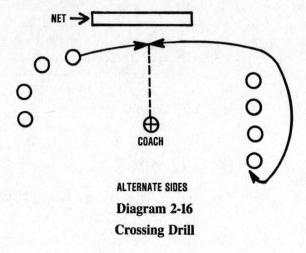

NET →

COACH

ALTERNATE SIDES

Diagram 2-16

Crossing Drill

We will continue in the same manner except that the receivers will come from opposite directions at the same time. The man in front will have his hands up and drop them to let the ball go through for the man in back to catch. This is an excellent concentration drill, as the man in front provides a distraction. Sides are alternated and each receiver gets two shots from each side.

We then go back to the individual crossing drill and throw low passes. We want the receiver to make the catch and take a good roll on the ground.

We form groups of three and the coach lobs the ball up and the three players go up for the ball and fight for it just as they would a basketball rebound.

We then have three receivers face the net and pair up with three ends who serve as passers. Each passer delivers a series of passes, aimed at alternating sides of the receiver. When the ball is delivered, the passer yells "ball" and the receiver turns on command, locates the ball, and makes the catch. This is an excellent concentration drill.

The receivers can simulate catching while running away from the passer by facing the net and running in place, looking back at the passers, and making an over-the-shoulder catch.

The receiver drills are covered every other day during the pre-season and at least once each week during the season.

DOUBLE TEAM

Blockers who are assigned to double team are drilled together so that they may execute this block in the individual period. Time in the practice schedule is set aside during the individual period for the various double team groups to work together. As an example, the tackles and ends will work together on the double. The end coach may work with the ends and tackles on one side of the line, while the tackle coach may work with the unit from the other side of the line. We do a great deal of double teaming for the ends and tackles and the wingbacks and ends, but much less for the other linemen. As a result, we devote much more practice time to the doubles we use the most. We do these kinds of doubles every day in pre-season, carrying out tackle-end doubles one day and wingback-end doubles the following day. During the season, we practice the kind of double that we expect to see in a given week from a particular opponent.

Doubles are taught in one or two groups of three. Initially, we have a defender hold a shield, but after doing this twice in the early practices, the double team drills scheduled for the individual periods are done live. We wish to drive the defender off the ball as far as possible. If we can also turn him with our double, that is a bonus. Our theory is contrary to that of many coaches who want to turn the defender and drive him laterally down the line of scrimmage. To accomplish our double, we have the post man make a drive block with the inside hip of the down lineman or the inside armpit of the linebacker as the target. The drive man will target the near hip of the defender (if he is a lineman) or the near armpit of the linebacker.

When we perfect the double team, we will work on doubling slanting or moving lineman (Diagram 2-17).

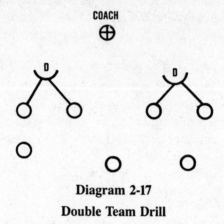

Diagram 2-17

Double Team Drill

CROSS BLOCK

We use some cross blocking in our offense. We schedule some time in our individual periods in the pre-season when ends and tackles must work together by having the two position coaches split the sides of the line. If other linemen cross block, time must be made for them to work on it during the individual offensive drill period. We practice the cross blocks in the individual periods at least once during game week if we anticipate using the block in the game.

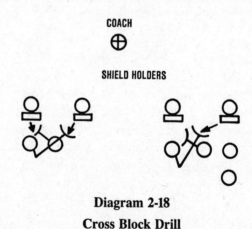

Diagram 2-18

Cross Block Drill

We do this with shields quite a bit, and occasionally live. We must get a realistic reaction from the shields so we have the outside defender close down and the inside defender penetrate, making the toughest possible blocking situation (Diagram 2-18).

LOOP

Our definition of the loop is the scheme in which a lineman must block down while the next man inside pulls around and picks up a scraping linebacker. The inside blocker must eyeball the defender all the way on the maneuver in order to make an adjustment on the move. Guards and tackles do most of this work for us, but other combinations are also used to a limited extent. A typical setup would have a guard coach work with one side and a tackle coach work with the other side. This is usually done with shields (Diagram 2-19). We go over this about four times during the pre-season and at least once during the week of a game in which we expect to use it.

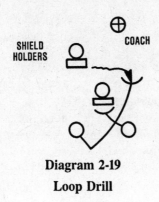

Diagram 2-19

Loop Drill

FOLD

Our definition of fold is for a lineman to drive through the near hip of a defensive lineman stationed to his outside, while the offensive lineman to his outside hitches and drives through a linebacker. Again, the drill must be scheduled during part of the individual period and broken down as to each side of the line. It is generally done with shields. We do not fold a great deal; therefore, we only practice it twice during the pre-season and, during the season, only when we expect to use it in a particular game (Diagram 2-20).

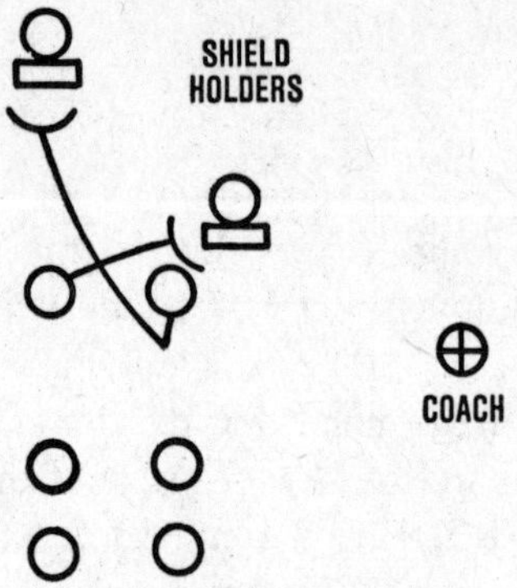

Diagram 2-20
Fold Drill

HIT AND RUN

Because of the gap stacks and near stacks in modern football, this block has become a necessity and one that we have found ourselves using more frequently each season. We do this every other day in the pre-season, breaking it down so that the center-guard, guard-tackle and tackle-end all get shots. We do it more with guard-tackles than the others. In game weeks we try to drill it for the groups that we expect to use it; at least once for the individual period is scheduled. It is not possible to become proficient at this critical scheme by putting it on the blackboard and then perfecting it in a group or team drill. (Do not repeat this early mistake that I made.) The transition from blackboard to group and team drill for the hit and run must be made in the individual period.

Our concept of the block is that the outside blocker will make a high drive block, targeting on the near armpit of the lineman to the inside, then bouncing off to the linebacker; the inside lineman targets the defensive lineman's outside hip. The bounce by the outside lineman will help the inside man successfully complete his block. The drill is done live about as often as it is with shields (Diagram 2-21).

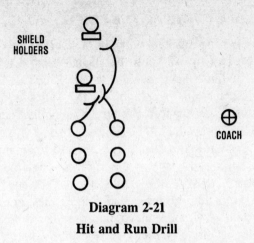

Diagram 2-21

Hit and Run Drill

COMBO

A combo means a change in assignments with an overblock by the inside man and a block on a linebacker by the outside man. We do this about twice in the pre-season and when we think it is approrpriate during the season. This is done with shields. The lineman holding the shield attempts to make a good penetration, making an excellent overblock necessary. The outside blocker drives directly for the outside armpit of the linebacker, making sure to anticipate leading him. The blocker taking the lineman is targeting the outside hip (Diagram 2-22).

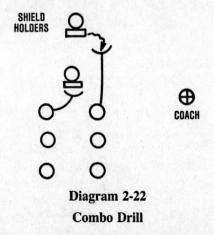

Diagram 2-22

Combo Drill

WEDGE THE STACK

With a stunting stack directly on a lineman, we sometimes block three on two by wedging the stack. Prior to adopting this scheme, the stunting stacks give us fits. In using this method, we double the lineman and single block the stunting or shuffling linebacker. It is necessary to break up the individual period so this can be done in groups of three adjacent linemen, either center-guard-tackle or guard-tackle-end. The covered lineman targets the inside hip of the lineman, attempting to run through the block. The outside lineman steps at the down lineman, then squares the shoulders and runs through the outside hip. If the hip is stationary, the block becomes a hit and run on the linebacker; if the hip is going inside, the blocker drives directly for the linebacker; if the hip is coming to the blocker, he drive blocks the lineman all the way. The

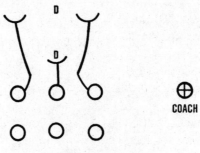

Diagram 2-23
Wedging the Stationary Stack

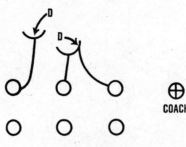

Diagram 2-24
Wedging the Stunting Stack

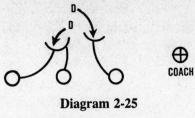

Diagram 2-25

Wedging the Stunting Stack

inside lineman carries out the same procedure with the inside hip. This drill is almost always done live (Diagrams 2-23, 2-24, and 2-25).

SEAL

One year we made an in-depth study of our game films in the off-season and found that backside defensive linemen were making almost fifty percent of the tackles against us. We just could not afford to allow penetration on the backside. Since we wanted our center to come frontside so much, we had to seal the backside to break the penetration. The technique for the down block and the seal block are exactly the same, so we have actually covered the seal in the everyday phase of individual drills. On the early days of pre-season and at infrequent intervals during the season, we feel it is necessary to go through a seal maneuver on a lineman who is reacting to the inside a bit more quickly than one who is being

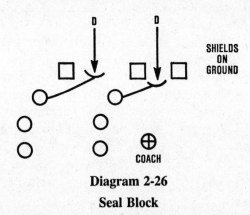

Diagram 2-26

Seal Block

blocked down. We do this drill live and have the defensive player
attempt to penetrate at an angle inside then then pursue down the
line. The seal must be excellent in order to cut him off (Diagram
2-26).

CROSSFIELD

Ends do a great deal of crossfield work. In our scheme, any
lineman who is assigned a seal and does not encounter resistance
will then execute a crossfield block. The crossfield block that we
teach is a drive block. We do not teach the roll or long body block.
The path crossfield is about five yards deep and aimed at the
extended hole of the play. The blocker is coached not to look for the
ball carrier. If he does that he will never make his block.

We have a defender hold a shield while the blocker searches
him out. We use this drill three times during the pre-season and
every other week during the season, as we think there is enough
crossfield work during dummy and actual scrimmage.

Any time we have an offensive practice, we go through starts
by driving off straight ahead, three times stepping with the right foot
first and three times stepping with the left foot first. We start three
times at a forty-five degree angle to the right and three times at a
forty-five degree angle to the left. We start three times both ways
directly down the line of scrimmage. We use the six-point hit out,
the drive block on down linemen directly on and slightly offset, the
down block, blocks on blitzing and flowing linebackers, and
individual pass protection drills. These make up the basis of our
offensive fundamentals and must be reviewed at every possible
opportunity. The other individual offensive line drills are designed
for coaching a particular maneuver for use during game week, or
brushing up on something that we have found lacking.

By saving all of the practice schedules, it is easy to see how
much time has been used for each phase of offensive line play. An
analysis can be made to better budget the time as the season
progresses. Practice should be planned so that the sequence of drills
can be performed efficiently. An example is to have ends and tackles
work cross blocks as well as doubles when they are scheduled to
work together.

THREE

Coaching Offensive Backs with Individual Drills

I have learned that the offensive position that must be filled first is the running back. A reasonably good athlete who will work diligently can learn to be an adequate quarterback and the team can succeed, but few teams will succeed without at least one very good running back.

The ability to elude tacklers is primarily innate. It can be enhanced to some degree by good drill work in tackling traffic, but you must seek out backs who can cut and accelerate quickly into an open area. Good coaching will produce offensive running backs who can block well, fake well, who seldom fumble, and who run very hard. Teams whose backs do these things consistently well year after year are not necessarily lucky; their backs are well coached. There are literally hundreds of fancy cutting and stepping drills for the running backs. After hundreds of hours of film study, I have concluded that most cutting and maneuvering drills are superfluous. Since the only way to be consistently good is to be fundamentally good, we attempt to make a strong case for the drills that insure the fundamentals.

STANCE

We usually divide the backs into three groups: (1) the running backs, (2) the wingbacks, and (3) the quarterbacks. You can combine these groups for many of the drills if you do not have enough coaches. We will cover the quarterback drills in the next chapter. On the first practice day, the running backs and wingbacks stretch and then learn the stance as their first drill. They review the drill on the second offensive day. We eliminate the drill after that, since we expect the coach to correct any stance problems in the other individual drills, group work, or teamwork to follow.

The backs align in a three-by three formation or as close to that as personnel will allow. The coach directs and instructs them as to the stance. Running backs and wingbacks should take a three-point stance with the feet nearly parallel and almost no weight forward. The coach instructs them to spread their feet about shoulder width apart and to place the fingers of the right hand on the ground slightly inside the right knee. The heel cleats are barely out of the ground and the back is straight with little weight on the hand. The left wrist rests on the left thigh. If the player wishes, he may assume a left-handed stance.

Tailbacks generally have an upright stance. In our offense either the wingback or one of the running backs could assume a tailback position. We have the tailback spread his feet about shoulder width and place his hands slightly above the knees, with his feet flat on the ground.

Sometimes the wingbacks play as a wide flanker, which alters the stance to one in which the inside foot is slightly back with hands on the hips and the weight on the balls of the feet.

STARTS

You can take two running backs with the same size and ability, but if one is significantly quicker in starting than the other, it will mean a great deal of difference in the manner in which they perform. It is truly difficult to overemphasize the importance of efficient starting for the running backs.

The backs are arranged in groups of three and assume the stance. The coach starts them with a cadence. There are three straight ahead starts stepping with the right foot first, three with the left foot first, three at a forty-five degree angle to the right with the right foot first, three at a forty-five degree angle to the left with the left foot first, three at a ninety degree angle flat down the line with the right foot first, and three at a ninety degree angle to the left down the line with the left foot first. Backs who assume more than one stance will alternate stances.

Starts are covered every day in the pre-season and twice each week in the individual periods in game week. The backs are also given starts on pre-game day and in the pre-game warm-up. As with linemen, it is a period that demands great concentration. A good coaching point is that the back must align in the proper stance and step with the proper foot in the proper direction. He is instructed to mentally put all his weight on the push-off foot and step first with the opposite foot. The back must start quickly if the offense is going to recognize its potential.

BALL EXCHANGE

Fumbles are the bane of a coach's existence. We have analyzed every game fumble for a period of five years and the vast majority of our ball exchange fumbles were caused by a poor reception pocket by the receiving back. If the back is presenting a poor pocket in game situations, you can bet that he has executed this same fundamental in a sloppy manner in practice—caused by poor concentration.

This drill is done every day in the first week of pre-season drills and twice in the second week. It is done only during the season when we think it is necessary. We do not feel that it is vital to do the drill every time we have individual offensive work because there is so much ball exchange work done in the offensive group and team drills.

The backs are aligned in two facing lines. A back presents the ball and hands it to a back coming the opposite way, who continues and hands it to a back going opposite his path. After the exchange, each back goes to the rear of the opposite line. Do not let this become a speed drill, as it is an initial coaching drill designed to acclimatize the backs to making a pocket and receiving the handoff properly. It is easy for the players to get too eager and start rushing this drill.

We instruct the handoff receiver to hold the inside arm up to the top of the numerals and the other arm at belt level with both forearms parallel to the ground. In a few days we expect the back to no longer look for the ball, but to close the upper arm down when the ball is inserted into his "pocket." The player handing off will feather the ball into the pocket with the lead hand.

HIGH STEPPING DRILLS

There have been some truly gifted running backs, such as Simpson and Sayers, who did not get their feet very far off the ground. These great backs had remarkable foot quickness and could cut quickly since their feet were always close to the ground. Nevertheless, we learned that backs who go down too easily usually do so because of bad balance or bad leg action. Drills to encourage high knee action can develop the back into a runner who drives his legs through arm tackles and does not trip easily as a result of the swipe at the ankles. Good high knee action also encourages good balance, causing the runner not to overextend his body and fall forward.

We utilize a device that is tubular and sits on legs about one foot off the ground. Rods protrude about eighteen inches from the sides of the device and are spaced about three feet apart. Running ropes can also be used for high stepping drills.

The first high stepping drill is done every time we have individual offensive drills, which translates to every day in the pre-season and twice each week during the season. Each back holds the ball properly with both hands and depresses his hips and high steps over the "snake." The device is forty feet in length. Each player goes down and back once (Diagram 3-1). We want the ball secured so that the index and thumb of each hand encircle the tips of each end of the ball. It is important that each player have his hips depressed, otherwise he will fail to generate the desired power in his running.

A second phase of the high stepping is the crossing over, now with the ball carried in one hand. This gets the hips rolling and

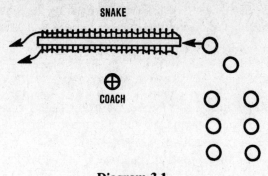

Diagram 3-1

High Stepping Over Snake

loosens them. The ball is carried with the index finger and thumb of one hand encircling the tip while the other tip is tightly lodged into the armpit. (The elbow must be in tight to the body.) The feet land on opposite sides of the snake. A trip down and back will suffice.

A specific phase of the high stepping work which we do on occasion is to hop over the rods with both feet and carry the ball with two hands. This is good for the ankles and gives the players explosive leg action.

CARRY DRILLS

A number of years ago we were evaluating our running backs after a scrimmage against another team and concluded that our runners went down much too easily on tackles from behind. We saw the need for the carry drills.

Good backs drag tacklers for many extra yards. To inspire our backs to do this, we use the carry drills. Each back has another back grab the belt at the back of his pants, digs in his cleats, and is carried a distance of fifteen yards. We ask the man being carried to really dig in and offer resistance so the ball carrier has to utilize good body lean and leg drive. The backs are split in half for the drill and switch positions on the way back.

The other carry drill involves the rider placing his upper arms in front and over the shoulders of the ball carrier and digging in his cleats. After fifteen yards, the pairs return with the roles being reversed. We use the carry drills every day during the first two weeks and once each week during the season.

RESISTANCE DRILLS

It is surprising how many teams neglect the fundamentals of hard running. I must also plead guilty to this oversight for many of my early years of coaching. Resistance drills are the core of our running back training program. Each back can be taught to generate more power in his running, to establish a stable center of gravity, and *to keep his legs moving.*

The first resistance drill incorporates the "snake," two shield holders, and a coach, player, or manager who acts as quarterback. The runner takes the handoff, proceeds about halfway up the snake with high knee action where he encounters the two shields and blasts between them. The shield holders offer a moderate amount of resistance early in the pre-season, then gradually increase the "shot" they give back until they are blasting as hard as possible by the second week of pre-season drills (Diagram 3-2). The ball carrier replaces one of the shield men, while the shield man rotates to the other shield spot, and the remaining shield holder goes to to the rear of the ball carrier line. The hips must be low and the ball carrier's chin cannot be very far in front of his feet, otherwise he will stumble and fall when he clears the resistance. The ball is held securely with

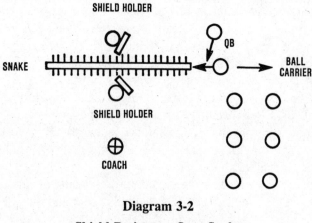

Diagram 3-2

Shield Resistance Over Snake

both hands and the knees are high. Each player gets three shots. This drill is done every day in the pre-season and twice each week during the season.

The second phase of the resistance drills has the "quarterback" and a coach or player holding a heavy dummy and striking the ball carrier at the shoulders with the swinging dummy as he proceeds up the "snake." It is easy to see the player stop his leg drive on the contact with the heavy dummy. With repeated work in the drill, improvement will come. The hips must be low, knees high, and the ball held securely with both hands (Diagram 3-3). Each player gets three shots. We do not begin this phase until the fourth day of pre-season practice. We then do it every day in the pre-season and twice each week during the season. There are a few times when we may skip the drill if we feel we are a bit too "banged up."

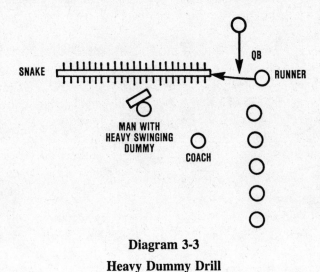

Diagram 3-3

Heavy Dummy Drill

Another phase of the drill is to station the "quarterback," two shield holders, and a swinging dummy holder on the snake. This is a very tough drill and should be used sparingly. Each player gets two shots.

PASS BLOCK

It seems as though we have much more trouble getting effective pass blocking from our backs than from our linemen. We have managed to improve our backs' pass blocking as a result of our development of game-tested drills for them.

The wingbacks do not pass block so they do not participate in this drill. The running backs are arranged so that a defender who is holding a shield will charge the running back. The back gets his hips down low and takes a short hard step at the defender as he closes. This step is necessary as the defender has gathered more momentum than a lineman would in a confrontation on the line of scrimmage. With the step forward, the back will thrust out his hands into the chest of the rusher, attempting to knock him off. If the defender attempts to grab the blocker (Diagram 3-4), he will knock his arms

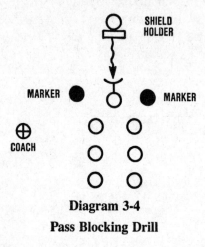

Diagram 3-4

Pass Blocking Drill

off with his hands. The blocker must shuffle and stay in front of the rusher, establishing a line from his nose through his back to the passer. If the blocker stops the charge of the rusher, he need not step at him again. Instead he will block as an offensive lineman would, remaining in the hitting position, striking out with the hands, attempting to establish and maintain separation with the rusher. If the rusher should gain position on the blocker, the back would then execute a down block by driving through the far hip of the rusher (Diagram 3-5). We use the shield the first two days of the drill, and do it live from then on. This drill is done every day in the pre-season and once each week during the season.

An aggressive pass block is used on action passes and sprint outs. It is drilled each day in the pre-season and once each week

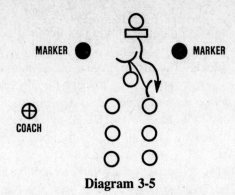

Diagram 3-5

Drive Block on Rusher When Position Is Lost

during the season. We align by using a cone marker for the position of the ball and another marker for the position of the tight end. The backs drive out to a point three yards outside the tight end's alignment and block aggressively against the penetrating pass defenders who are holding shields. After the first two sessions, we alternate going live with using the dummy in this drill. Each blocker gets two shots in each direction (Diagram 3-6).

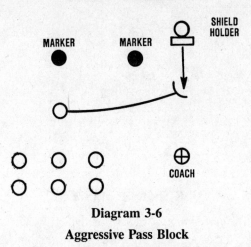

Diagram 3-6

Aggressive Pass Block

LEAD BLOCK

Before we started making this block effectively, we recognized that we had to mark a channel for the blocker to run through and we had to school a defender to stuff the play with force. We found that the defender had to go through a progression of harder charges for the blocker to gain confidence in taking on the tough defenders in a live situation.

The lead block is used for power plays in the offense and directs a back to block after running through the line leading another back. We set two cones and have a defender holding a shield. The blocker drives through the cones (Diagram 3-7) and targets the armpit of the defender. He must have his body under control in making the block. The hips are down and the blocker is not generating all of his speed. He is instructed to run through the target. The shield holder will step forward and blast the blocker with the shield and offer as much resistance as he can. We do the drill every other day in the pre-season and about once every two weeks during the season, as we do not use the block as much as the kick-out or sweep block. We do the drill live about twice in the pre-season but seldom live during the season. Each player gets about three shots.

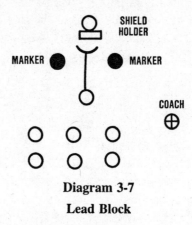

Diagram 3-7

Lead Block

KICK-OUT BLOCK

This is the *fundamental* block for the off tackle offense. (We started making the block well after we discovered our lead back was not getting a proper angle to make the block.) We must get upfield position on the defender or the block does not work. We target the inside armpit of the defender, but if the defender is upfield we do not need a block (he has run himself out of the play and created a seam).

If we run through the inside armpit, it will be a shoulder block. When the defender closes, it may not be possible to get through the inside armpit, in which case we log the defender and get as close to the target as possible.

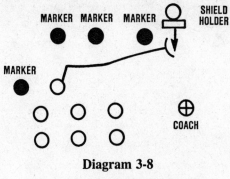

Diagram 3-8
Kick Out Drill—Initial Set-Up

We mark the position of the ball and the position of the tight end and station a defender with a shield (Diagram 3-8) outside the tight end. The blocker must run the proper route in order to get an inside out angle on the end. He steps up towards the second marker on the ground (there is a first market to align the blocker's starting position) for two steps, then drives for the end, aiming for the near armpit. To begin the progression, we have the end penetrate so the blocker can make his contact and carry out the "ideal" block. He must be under control and have his hips down so he can keep his feet moving. The most common mistake on the block is the tendency to overextend with the chin way out in front of the feet which will cause the blocker to go the ground. The blocker should literally run through by stepping on the toes of the target. The second day we repeat the initial phase, then have the end remain on the line of scrimmage, presenting a less inviting target for our fullback (Diagram 3-9). We repeat the process the third day. The fourth day we have the end close down on the block, playing it very low, making it necessary for the fullback to log or bury the defender, which causes the ball carrier to adjust his path (Diagram 3-10). We do the drill every time we practice offense, throughout the season.

We seldom do it live once the season begins, but there are times when we feel we must "toughen up" and execute the drill live.

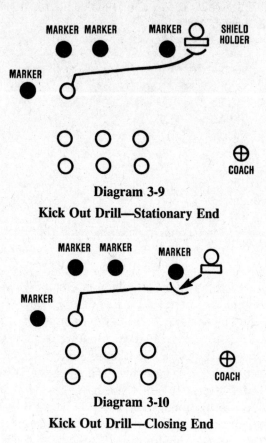

Diagram 3-9

Kick Out Drill—Stationary End

Diagram 3-10

Kick Out Drill—Closing End

FILL BLOCK

We have experienced breakdowns in some cases when we have asked backs to fill-in for pulling or double teaming linemen. The tendency on the part of the back is to tiptoe up to the hole and avoid contact. If we teach the drill properly on an individual basis in the early season, and insist that the maneuver be carried out properly in all succeeding group and team drills, we have good success with the fill block.

The drill to teach the block in the individual period is installed on the day the play involving the fill maneuver is to be taught. It is repeated twice in the pre-season and rarely during the season. We station two markers, the blocker drives out from a stance and targets the inside armpit of the defender. The defender penetrates through the gap, doing so slowly and easily at first, progressing to a quicker, closing penetration as the drill proceeds (Diagram 3-11).

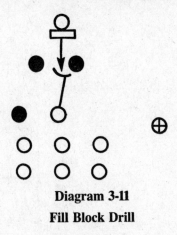

Diagram 3-11

Fill Block Drill

SWEEP BLOCK

In designing an effective individual drill for the sweep block, we were confronted with the problem of blocking all the possibilities that we would encounter against a fluid container, with setting up the teaching progression so as to build confidence and gain competence, and with making the drill one that minimized the possibility of injury. Since the block is important in our offense, the construction of the drill was critical.

We pair up a runner with a blocker and set up two markers and a shield holder upfield from the markers. A blocker and the ball carrier begin the sweep course. Initially, the shield holder is somewhat passive but he picks up intensity as the blocker refines technique (Diagram 3-12). The ball carrier and the blocker are instructed to run an arc, with the ball carrier a yard behind and a yard outside the blocker. The arc is prescribed by the markers. If the arc is broken by the defender, the blocker will target a block on the inside armpit and the ball carrier will cut to the inside (Diagram

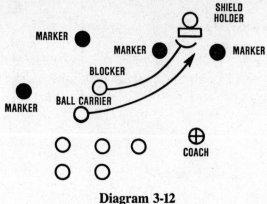

Diagram 3-12

Sweep Block Drill—Initial Phase

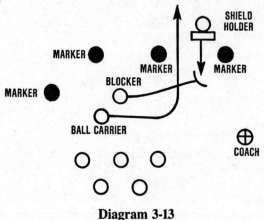

Diagram 3-13

Sweep Block Drill—Arc Broken

3-13), making a slight deviation. If the arc to be described by the blocker is unbroken, the ball carrier will remain on the blocker's hip and run upfield. The blocker will turn upfield until the defender is about to cross the arc; at that point the blocker turns his eyes inside and runs through the outside knee of the defender. It is not a rolling block, but a shoulder dip and a run through the target (Diagram 3-14). If the block is properly executed, the defender will be on the ground.

This drill is practiced with shields for the first few times, with

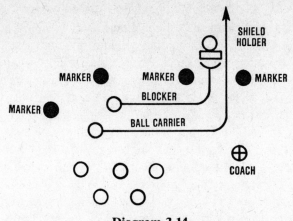

Diagram 3-14

Sweep Block-Running Through Outside Knee

the shield holder penetrating the arc at various points. We then go through the drill live for the remainder of the pre-season, doing it live occasionally during the season. We do the drill every day in the pre-season and once each week during the regulation season.

RECEIVING DRILLS

Receiver drills are practiced by wingbacks three times each week during the pre-season. We would like to have time to do them twice each week during the season, but we can only get them in once every other week because of our priorities. Running backs catch tosses, pitch-outs, and occasionally passes, so we see that they are exposed to receiver drills twice in the pre-season but only occasionally during the season.

WING BLOCKS

The set of the tight wing will make some of his blocking assignments and techniques unique to him. The teaching and repetitive drills used for individual work must be set up to develop the skills needed to make his blocks successfully.

We coach the wings to make the drive block on the double team, the single block on a containing defender, a clear through and wall off on a linebacker, a delayed sweep block, and a crossfield block. The wing's double team is in conjunction with the end. We practice this double every other day in the pre-season and once a week when we anticipate the double during the season. The block is taught against a defender holding a shield, then practiced live.

In using the single block, the wing is taught to come off the ball *softly* and under control, targeting the inside armpit of the defender. The objective is not to run the defender off the ball or to move him; but merely to occupy the opponent. We begin with a defender off the line holding a shield then more to a defender on the line. As time goes on, the defender can attempt to duck the blocker by moving in one direction or the other. We also have the defender close the blocker very hard at times. We do the drill without shields after a couple of days in the pre-season, then go back to shields for the season. The drill is done every day during the pre-season and once a week during the season.

At times we assign the wing to run through on a linebacker to his inside. Again, he comes off softly, turns and runs through the inside armpit of the target. He must be under control, since he is out in the open where there is plenty of room for the defender to maneuver. He is not expected to knock the linebacker down. We just want him to occupy the defender. The drill is set up with markers and the defender is supplied with a shield. We go through it every day in the pre-season, progressing to live work the second day, then once each week with shields during the season. In the normal progression of the drill, we have the shield holders attempt to duck the block and move around the wing, creating a game-like situation that he should be able to handle once he has developed confidence in the technique and has an understanding of what he is trying to accomplish.

The sweep block is practiced with a ball carrier and the same theory applies as it does when a back leads it out of the backfield (Diagram 3-15). The exception in technique is that the wing steps forward with his inside foot, delays and then commences his arc. The ball carrier will time up his path with the wing. The arc principle is still employed and the technique is exactly the same. Wings do not utilize this block as much as running backs and thus practice it every other day in the pre-season, the last week without shields and once each week against shields during the season if we plan to utilize the maneuver for the given week.

The wing is sometimes assigned to hook the contain man. The

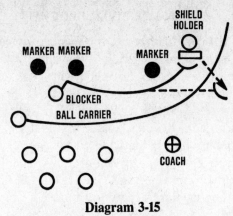

Diagram 3-15

Wing Leading Sweep

drill is set up with a shield and we have the blocker come off quickly and run through the outside hip of a close contain man. We also use the situation in which the contain man refuses to be hooked. When that is the case, the wing comes off softly, gets into the inside armpit of the defender and runs with him to the outside, which redirects the play to the inside (Diagram 3-16). We drill the hook twice in the pre-season and only once during weeks in which we plan to use the play involving the block. We do it with shields most of the time.

Wings do crossfield work and are drilled on it with the same drill that we use for ends. We only use the drill to teach the block twice during the pre-season and do not use it after that. We depend on dummy scrimmage work to keep us sharp in making the block.

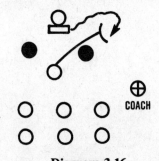

Diagram 3-16

Wing Riding Contain Man Out

WIDE RECEIVER BLOCKS

The "wide outs" that are used in modern football incorporate new concepts in blocking because of the manner in which they are defensed. We structured our drills for wide receiver blocking to reflect the defensive situations we were seeing in games. Wide receiver blocks are: the stalk block, the clear across the hole, the slow crackback block, the crossfield block, and the cutoff block.

Stalk blocking directs the wide out to step off directly at the defender covering him. The play is a wide play and the objective is to keep the defender from closing it. We begin with shields without a ball carrier and on the third day we incorporate a ball carrier and do it live. The drill is done five times during the pre-season and once each week during the season if we are to use it that week. The blocker must come off under control, attempting to run off the coverage man. The defender will initially yield about four or five steps, then stop and head back towards the line. The blocker is responsible for reading the defender and executes a pass protection block on him when he begins forward motion. The blocker attempts to occupy the defender as long as he can (Diagram 3-17). If the defender gains position, the receiver drive blocks the far armpit of the defender. The second phase of the drill has the shield holder remaining in position and not backpedaling, which means the blocker must break down sooner and make his block slightly more

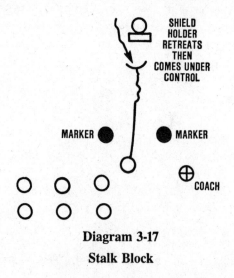

Diagram 3-17

Stalk Block

aggressive (Diagram 3-18). In the third phase, the coverage man is up tight on the nose of the wide receiver, who makes a soft drive block through the armpit, in the same manner the wing blocks the single container, except this block must be sustained for a longer period of time (Diagram 3-19).

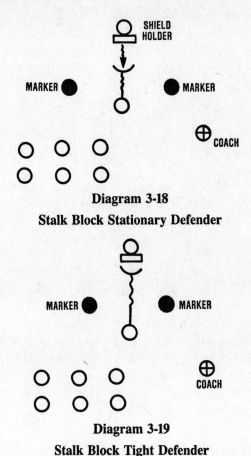

Diagram 3-18

Stalk Block Stationary Defender

Diagram 3-19

Stalk Block Tight Defender

There is a fourth phase for the stalk block, in which the defender is coming up quickly with a sharp move to the inside. This takes some work and the use of good judgment on the part of the blocker. We want the blocker to make a beeline to block the defender. He must gauge whether or not he can make the block legally (above the waist and without clipping); if not he must resume his upfield course and stalk a deeper defender (there is usually a safety swinging over if a defender on the corner is rolling up). If he can get to the man rolling up, the blocker must make his aggressive block on the near armpit (Diagram 3-20).

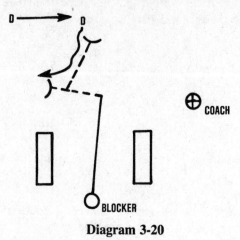

Diagram 3-20

Stalk Block Defender Rolling Up-Inside

Wide receivers are also asked to clear across the hole on off tackle plays. The wide receiver steps to the inside quickly from his position, driving across the hole at a depth of six yards from the line of scrimmage. His duty is to clear anything in his path. We use shields for the drill and do not run it live in the individual period. It is run every other day in the pre-season and once in weeks in which we plan to use it in the game. Markers are set and the shield holder is assigned.

The blocker comes inside hard and drives right for the shield. He slows up by dropping his hips as he approaches the shield. He has to judge his course and speed, gaining skill in these facets of the operation with repeated drills. As the drill progresses, shield holders are coached to take evasive maneuvers, making it tougher for the blocker to execute the inside armpit block.

The slow crackback block is used on sweeps and involves a certain amount of reading by the blocker. Two shield holders are arranged by markers (Diagram 3-21). The blocker comes slowly down the line of scrimmage as flat as he can. If the defender assigned to contain is coming out quickly to make the play, the

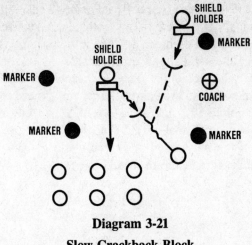

Diagram 3-21

Slow Crackback Block

defender walls him off with a block on the inside armpit (all blocks must be made above the waist if from outside in and in the vicinity of the scrimmage). If the blocker sees that the defender has penetrated too quickly for him to make a legal block, or sees that he does not need to block the container, the wide receiver releases on the coverage man and runs through the outside armpit. The coach instructs the container on which action to take and the drill simulates game conditions. We do the drill three times in the pre-season and once during weeks that the block is anticipated as part of the game plan.

The cutoff block is used when the play is a quick hitter in the middle. We would not use the crossfield block in this situation since we think there is a good chance the play could break to the outside after it crosses the line of scrimmage. We do not wish to take a sharp inside route so we do not drag the defender inside. Consequently, the wide receiver pushes off for the inside leg of the defender covering. We want him to run hard and attempt to adjust his path so he can get to the inside armpit of the defender. There is no slowing up for this block. If the defender makes our man miss, we just attempt to recover and block someone else. The concept is to keep the defender from closing the play vertically and simultaneously squeezing it to the inside. If the defender does make the quick evasive move to the inside, the good ball carrier makes an outside cut; otherwise, the properly executed cutoff gives our back enough cushion to get deep into the secondary and possibly run by the defender. We set the drill by using markers and a shield holder. In the progression, we have the defender alternating the quick inside move with the soft squeezing and closing action. The blocker will be unable to make the block in the first situation and will make it in the second situation if the shield holder is doing a good job. This recreates the game situation for our individual period (Diagram 3-22). We do the drill three times in the pre-season and once a week in game weeks in which we think we will see the situation.

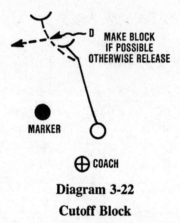

Diagram 3-22

Cutoff Block

All backs are drilled on starts in every individual offensive drill, going straight ahead three times with the left foot first then the right foot first, three times at a forty-five degree angle to the right, three times at a forty-five degree angle to the left, three times at a ninety degree angle down the line left, and three times at a ninety degree angle down the line right. Each back does high stepping drills over the "snake" every offensive day. We do "carry" drills every offensive day. At least one kind of resistance drill is done every time we have individual offensive drills. Fullbacks do kick out blocks every time we practice offense. Other drills are blended in as mentioned in this chapter.

FOUR

Developing The Quarterback with Game-Tested Drills

Many coaches use the best available athlete at quarterback, but you are depending on luck if you expect a super athlete to come along each year as your "trigger man." Coaching a consistent offense means taking the prospective quarterback and polishing his natural skills so that he will be a proficient ball handler, runner, and passer. The basic credentials for the position include: relatively good foot movement, eye-hand coordination, and arm-shoulder flexibility. Size, a sense of timing, speed, and strength are ingredients that separate the "mechanics" from the "artists."

BALL EXCHANGE DRILL

There is no excuse for a fumble on the center-quarterback exchange. The first and most fundamental thing that the quarterback does is take the snap from the center. If you have trouble, think about how effectively you taught and drilled this fundamental in the early part of the pre-season. Poor habits and sloppiness here will lead to problems throughout the season.

We utilize this drill only in the pre-season and immediately after the stretching period. We like to work in sets of threes with both quarterback and center coaches directing the activity. Initially, we will work the first team quarterback with the first team center, second team quarterback and center together, and so on, but as time goes on we like to familiarize all the quarterbacks with all the centers. We assign a quarterback to call out the cadence for all members of the group. Each center aligns with a ball. For right-handed quarterbacks, we put the laces to the right and the center places his hands on the ball so the thumbs are nearly together and run along the top seam. The quarterback has his thumbs together and up with the fingers spread, exerting pressure against the buttocks of the center. This is an old-fashioned way to take the exchange but one that we like. If the pressure is against the buttocks, the hands of the quarterback will automatically follow the center as he steps to make his block. The fingers automatically close on the ball when it strikes the quarterback's hands. Each center is instructed to step with the right foot first three times. On the first day of the drill, the quarterbacks receive the exchange and seat the ball by bringing it to the "third hand," the midsection. Quarterbacks take turns calling cadence (Diagram 4-1).

On the second day of the drill, the quarterbacks go through their footwork for plays that they learned in the previous practice. The centers step with the foot in the direction that the assigned play dictates.

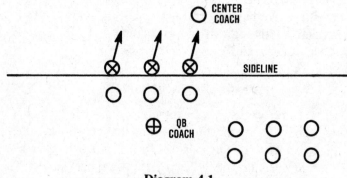

Diagram 4-1
Initial Center-Quarterback Exchanges

Later on in the first week of practice, the quarterbacks will take their pivots, while the centers are assigned to block shields after going through the starts initially. We do not use the exchange drills after the pre-season.

BALL HANDLING DRILLS

A quarterback puts the ball in play for every offensive play. Consequently, the coach must drill him with the aim of developing quick hands and establishing muscle memory for the geometry of the football. Just as for any skill, repetition combined with concentration leads to perfection.

We align each quarterback on the sideline facing the coach (Diagrom 4-2). There is a football in front of each player. The quarterbacks are instructed to use the right hand to lift the ball from the ground as quickly as possible. The ball is then replaced on the ground and the cycle is completed. We strive for about ten rapidfire repetitions, then repeat the procedure with the left hand.

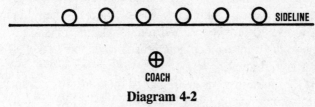

Diagram 4-2

Ball Handling Drills

The quarterbacks then hold the ball with the right hand so that the nose is down. They drop the ball and attempt a one-handed catch before it strikes the ground. After ten of these we repeat the drill with the left hand. We then perform the drop with the right hand, but the ball is held so that the long axis is parallel to the ground. This is also repeated with the left hand.

Finally, we perform the globetrotter drill in which the ball is passed through the legs from hand to hand as rapidly as possible for about thirty seconds. We will do the ball handling drills for every offensive drill period except on those days when it is extremely wet.

WARMING UP THE PASSING ARM

The purpose of these drills is to warm up the passing arm as well as to develop good technique. We spend some time during the first few practices carefully instructing the passers in the fundamentals of throwing the football, then dismiss with introductory instructions. After a few days, we proceed directly to the passing drills, encouraging the players by pointing out what they are doing well as well as correcting errors in form. In making corrections, we try to correct *one* thing at a time; it can be demoralizing and confusing to a player if the coach offers many corrections simultaneously.

We have the quarterback grip the ball so that his fingers are on the laces and as far up on the fat part of the ball as possible. If the individual's grip is too far up, there will not be any space visible between the palm and the ball. The throwing motion is preceded by holding the ball at the chest with the left hand on top. To execute the pass, the quarterback will simultaneously step in the direction of the target with the left foot and extend the ball behind the ear. We teach the passing motion as rotational and direct the passer to quickly turn his hips square to the direction of flight just as he releases the ball. We believe that this is a simple instruction that accomplishes the passing form we are looking for. The shoulders come square and the ball is delivered properly. Good rotational hip and shoulder action may cause the right-handed quarterback to fall off to the left slightly in his follow through.

If the quarterback is getting good rotation, we then spend some time in instructions on the follow through. We like the palm turned out and the arm to continue its trajectory to about the level of the player's waist. We prefer that the passer release the ball with the arm almost fully extended (an overhand motion), which should provide a

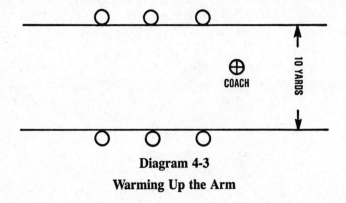

Diagram 4-3
Warming Up the Arm

little more leverage on the ball. However, we do not insist on this as there have been many fine passers with partial sidearm motions.

The first step in warming up the arms is to group the quarterbacks in two's and throw the ball back and forth within each group, playing a simple game of catch at a distance of ten yards (Diagram 4-3). We emphasize easy hip and shoulder rotation. Each passer gets about ten tosses.

We have each passer get down so his right knee is on the ground and have him pass the ball to his partner at the ten yard distance. This is a good opportunity to get the shoulders moving and rotating to the target, since the "legs" of the passer do not come into use. Each passer gets six tosses, then we have them try with both knees down for six tosses each, then with the left knee down for six passes each.

Next, we back up to a twenty yard distance and have the passers throw as hard as possible. We emphasize accuracy in the drill (aiming for the receiver's nose, as small a target as possible) and trying to keep the ball on a line. Each passer tries six passes.

We have each passer and his partner run the lines at a distance of ten yards. One trip up and back should be sufficient. Their distance apart is short enough so that the players can stay on the line, not stepping at the target, but letting the rotation of the hips do the work (Diagram 4-4).

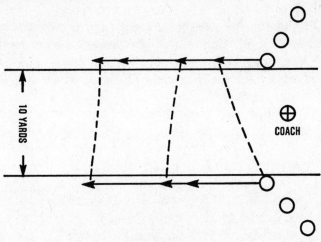

Diagram 4-4

Running the Lines—Quarterbacks

Each of the preceding arm warm up drills are carried out every time we practice offense.

A drill we do every other day in the pre-season but only rarely during the season is the circle drill in which markers construct a circle twenty yards in diameter and three players run clockwise, throwing the ball to the next man on the circle. When each player has made six throws, the group will run counterclockwise and repeat the process (Diagram 4-5). It is a drill similar to running the lines, but the different angle of release changes the problem enough to make the drill a valuable supplement.

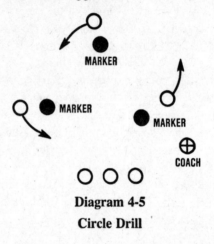

Diagram 4-5
Circle Drill

A drill we do every day in the pre-season but only rarely during the season is the step drill in which the passer has a ball and on the coach's command will step at the coach and extend his throwing arm but hold on to the ball. The coach will zigzag to different spots to insure that passers are stepping with the lead foot at the target.

Another drill used every other day in the pre-season and rarely during the season is the one in which a passer stands holding the ball ready at a distance of twenty yards from his partner. The coach barks out a "throw" command; the passer releases the ball as soon as he can, using proper throwing motion. This will aid the passer in getting the ball off quickly and impress him with the importance of keeping the ball up and ready.

Occasionally we have the passers throw a completed route pattern to another passer. We do not use this drill until the season is underway, and then only rarely. The passer throws any desired pattern to a partner who is standing at the spot where the completion should be (in relation to the quarterback's location) (Diagram 4-6). This gives the passer a concept of exactly where the target should be and teaches him to make his throw to that particular spot.

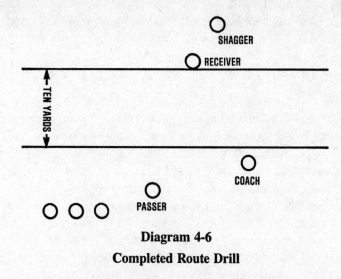

Diagram 4-6

Completed Route Drill

FOOTWORK BY THE NUMBERS

You simply cannot have an athlete with poor foot movement play any position in football; but footwork at quarterback is at a premium. You must start with a player with relatively good foot movement and then work to develop his footwork with "quick feet" drills and detailed, highly disciplined play work. The slow-footed and misstepping quarterback will destroy the timing of any offense and lead to losses and fumbles.

We do some portion of this work in every offensive individual drill period. In the pre-season, we very carefully go through the plays that are to be taught on the given day and review all plays learned in previous practice sessions. During the season, time does not permit us to go through all plays, but we select the ones in which footwork needs improvement.

We align all the quarterbacks on a sideline, each with a ball, facing the coach. The coach works on the first play to be taught for the day and demonstrates the quarterback footwork by the numbers, indicating the first step, the second step, and so on. He then has the quarterbacks go through each step, making the step as the coach calls out the number of the step, "one—two—three." After going through a play twice by the numbers, the coach selects one of the group to call the cadence, and all quarterbacks simultaneously carry out the mechanics of the play at full speed. The quarterbacks take turns in calling cadence, as several repetitions of each play are completed.

QUARTERBACKS IN THE BACKFIELD DRILL

We fell into this drill one day during pre-season when we had a little extra time at the end of the quarterback individual drill period. As a result we took the quarterbacks and had them play all the backfield positions and reviewed all the running plays. The quarterbacks commented that the drill forced them to learn the routes that the running backs must use. Since that time we have used the drill every other day in the pre-season and infrequently during the season. If you use this drill, your quarterbacks will gain a better "nuts and bolts" understanding of the offense—one that you cannot duplicate with hours of classroom or blackboard drills. In short, your quarterbacks will become more complete football players.

PITCH DRILLS

It seems as though it is difficult to watch a high school or college game in which there is not at least one bad pitch. Most of these errant tosses are the result of poor fundamental execution by the quarterback. It is necessary to teach and drill this phase of the game in the individual quarterback period.

Our offense utilizes three kinds of quarterback pitchouts. They are the tailback sweep pitch, the long belly pitch, and the quick pitch.

In the tailback sweep pitch, the quarterback puts his weight on his playside foot and reverse pivots, making a two-hand dead-ball pitch that leads the tailback. The quarterback completes his pivot and then runs a proper blocking route. We practice the pitch by stationing a partner behind each quarterback. One of the signal callers calls cadence and all simultaneously execute the pitch (Diagram 4-7). We alternate the cadence callers, and run the pitches in both directions.

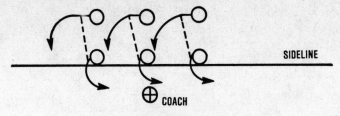

Diagram 4-7

Pitch Drill for Tailback Sweep

The long belly pitch is made after à ride to the fullback. Since the tailback is a good distance away from the quarterback when the pitch is made, we emphasize a two-hand basketball chest pass. A player and his partner are aligned seven yards apart at an oblique angle, and the pitches are executed back and forth. Each player gets six pitches, then positions are exchanged so that six pitches to the opposite side are made by each quarterback (Diagram 4-8).

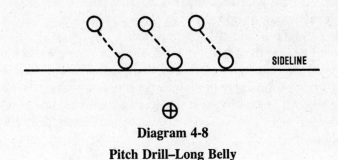

Diagram 4-8

Pitch Drill—Long Belly

The quick pitch drill is very similar to the belly pitch drill. The fundamental is executed by simply pushing off the back foot, extending the front foot, and extending the index fingers of both hands toward the target. This results in a two-hand underhand pitch that is a "dead" or non-rotating ball. It is a simple and quick toss. The quarterback simulates taking a snap but does not pull the ball to the waist. Instead, he makes the toss to the target that is not as far away as for the belly pitch. Each player should get six tosses in each direction.

OPTION DRILLS

We use the belly option and attempt to make a long ride fake to the fullback and then option the fourth man from inside out on the line of scrimmage. If the defender is *not* in the pitch lane or is *not* beating a rapid path to the outside, we coach the quarterback to execute the long belly pitch. If the two exceptions are met, the quarterback extends both hands, fakes the pitch, plants the outside foot, and carries the ball upfield himself. To make the "read" properly, the quarterback must be exposed to all situations in the individual, group, and team periods.

The drill is set up to include a quarterback, fullback, and a tailback, with another player assigned to hold a shield (playing the part of the man we will option). In the initial phases of the drill, the shield holder remains static, which calls for a pitch by the quarterback. Then we have the shield holder drive into the pitch lane, which calls for a keep by the quarterback. Next, we assign the shield holder to widen quickly, which also calls for the keep by the quarterback. The idea is to make the choice very obvious in order for the ball handler to gain confidence. We want to progress to the phase in which the man to be optioned mixes his charges so our quarterback needs to make the read without anticipating the defender's play. Once we believe the quarterback has adequately progressed through the initial stages of the drill, we have the defender mix the charges and be more subtle about the different charges, making them a bit more difficult to read. We alternate turns at all positions and work both sides. The quarterbacks fill all the positions for the drill (Diagram 4-9).

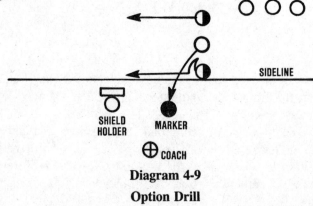

Diagram 4-9

Option Drill

INDIVIDUAL PATTERN DRILLS

We import a set of ends (one side only) or wingbacks plus a reserve center for this work. We prefer to work on one pattern at a time. The cadence is called and the quarterback takes the snap, sets up (or sprints out, bootlegs, etc.), and the receiver takes off into his pattern. The ball is delivered and the next group promptly moves in. We always have the receiver who has previously completed the pattern act as the "shagger" (Diagram 4-10). If he can be spared, an end or wingback coach can check the patterns carefully while the quarterback coach checks the set-up and throwing technique. We use this drill about four times in the pre-season and once each week in season. It is a good drill because it allows us to time-up specific patterns between passer and receiver, developing some confidence before we get other receivers, backs and defenders in the picture.

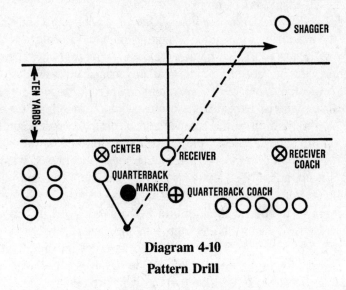

Diagram 4-10

Pattern Drill

HARD RUNNING DRILLS

These are the same drills the running backs use except we must abbreviate them for the quarterbacks. We pull and carry partners four times during the pre-season and occasionally during the season. The quarterbacks step over the snake every day during the pre-season and once each week in season. We do resistance drills on the snake about three or four times a season.

TACTICS AND STRATEGY DRILLS

If you have the quarterback calling the plays, you must spend a great deal of time and effort training him for this task. A single play is never an isolated entity; it always fits into the larger pattern or context of the strategic situation, or the game itself. The modern trend is for the coaching staff to call the plays by sending in substitutes or to signal visually to the quarterback from the sidelines. The choice of play is generally determined by coordination of spotters who are linked to the bench by telephones and who have developed a guide or game plan of which play to call for a specific situation. We call all our plays from the sideline or from upstairs, and initially we believed it was not necessary to give our quarterbacks any more than a perfunctory knowledge of play calling logic and direction. We subsequently decided that we were wrong in not training our quarterbacks more thoroughly.

Even the quarterback who has his plays called for him can profit enormously from good training in play calling for the following reasons: (1) The quarterback will function better if he is thinking with the coaching staff and understands the why of the "call," (2) the other squad members will gain respect for the quarterback who understands the offense and knows all the ins and outs, (3) it is helpful to the coaching staff to have someone on the field who is able to discuss the tactical situation and who has the "feel" of the game, and (4) the quarterback who knows what is going on can adjust formations, spacings, assignments, and make minor adjustments on the line of scrimmage.

Possibly the oldest strategy drill in the game is the blackboard drill. In the pre-season, the quarterbacks meet every day before the offensive practice. The off-season is also an excellent time for this drill. We try to go over each play on the day it is introduced and teach our quarterbacks the situations in which to use the play. This entails describing whether the play is based on deception or power, is a high or low consistency play (in our definition, high consistency plays are expected to gain four yards or more 50% of the time, whereas the low consistency plays do not meet that requirement but are expected to break for a gain of ten yards or better at least fifteen percent of the time), and what other plays this particular play would complement.

The blackboard drill is also used to establish a general over-the-field play-calling procedure. We prefer to go about this by exception, in other words, we tell the quarterbacks which plays not to call in certain down and distance, field, hash mark, time, weather, and score situations. On the day we introduce our "beat the clock" offense, we spend a great deal of time going over the procedure with the quarterbacks on the blackboard. We must make sure that the quarterbacks know the rules governing the stopping and starting of the clock.

During the season, the quarterbacks get a copy of the offensive game plan, which is one sheet of paper. They are expected to know which formations and plays will be used for the given week. When we distribute the game plan, we spend some time on the blackboard with the trigger men. This is done on Monday night after practice. Wednesday night after practice we have a blackboard drill for the quarterbacks—we simply put up different situations and defenses and have the quarterbacks make the calls. We find that they begin to anticipate our own calls.

It is very helpful to sit down and go over your own game film with the quarterbacks, explaining to them the reason for every play that was called. On a more advanced level, the coach can go over an opponent film with the quarterbacks and have the calls made for every tactical situation on the film according to the offensive game plan for that particular week.

DAILY ROUTINE

For every offensive practice the quarterbacks do all the ball handling drills, taking a few easy tosses at ten yards, throwing from one and both knees at a distance of ten yards, throwing hard at a distance of twenty yards, and running the lines throwing back and forth at a distance of ten yards. We always do some form of by-the-numbers play work. Play calling drills are scheduled every day in the pre-season and twice each week during the season. All other drills are scheduled if time allows and if needed.

FIVE

Coaching Offensive Group Work

DEVELOPING THE OFFENSIVE LINE THROUGH GROUP WORK

Quick Assignment Drill

Through analysis of film, the offensive coach will find that the greatest single cause of breakdown is the missed assignment. Knowing *whom* to block is the most important offensive fundamental in the game. Playbooks, good and flexible blocking rules, meaningful blackboard sessions, paper and pencil and oral tests—all are helpful, but none of these can take the place of actual on-the-field assignment work.

The quick assignment work is scheduled in the group phase of offensive practice for a time period of about nine minutes. New plays are emphasized against several different defenses. During the season the drill is scheduled and executed against expected opponent defenses for the week. Our objective is to cover outside and off tackle plays for the first five minutes, then send the ends to the backs for pass offense, while the interior line reviews the inside plays for about four minutes.

Shields are placed on the ground against a first offensive line, with seconds and thirds behind the first unit. The shields are aligned in the desired defensive front, including linebackers and linemen. Any variations in blocking assignments are discussed quickly, pointing out specific maneuvers against defensive faces. In game week it may be necessary to alter assignments because of kinds of charges, unusual spacings, or particular personnel of the opponent. The coach calls plays from the line and the players step toward assigned defenders. The plays can be run very rapidly in this manner. The second group will not need as much time as the first group for this work, since they have the advantage of observing the first unit. The third unit should see some part of the work also (Diagram 5-1).

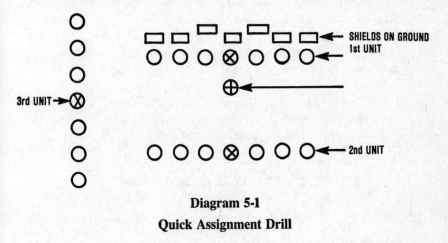

Diagram 5-1

Quick Assignment Drill

The coach must decide which defenses and which plays will be used prior to coming on the practice field. In the pre-season, the practice schedule will detail the new plays to be taught in the group period for the offensive line. During the season, the scouting report will determine which defenses to prepare. The coach must review the game plan thoroughly and any assignment differences must be decided before coming on the field. The drill can be easily evaluated while in progress. Mistakes must be corrected on the field.

Coaching Offensive Linemen With Shield Work

As previously indicated, blocking techniques can only be

mastered through correct repetition. Our stress is on (1) stepping with the proper foot, (2) stepping off with the count, (3) maintaining level body position, and (4) running through the target.

During offensive group periods, the entire offensive line repeats the fundamental shield drills that were accomplished in the preceding individual period. The purpose of such repetition is to train the line to assume position on a line of scrimmage as a unit, to carry out the drill at a game-like tempo, and to acclimatize the line to taking off as a unit.

First, the defenders line up just slightly behind the ball with the shields at knee level in order to simulate the position of a defensive lineman. The shields are directly in front of each blocker. The center passes the ball back to the coach. We use the drill on a lined field, but seldom place the ball on a marked line; this simulates game conditions. One unit holds the shields, while another participates in the offensive phase of the drill, with a unit observing. The drill progresses rapidly and the three groups rotate after each play. The drill is designed so that:

1. The line drives out and runs through the edge of the shield, which is held just off the ball and at knee height, then repeats this to the opposite side (Diagram 5-2).

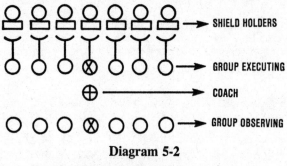

Diagram 5-2

Shield Drill, Defensive Lineman on Nose

2. The shield is offset slightly; the line drives out and makes contact at the outside hip, running through the target. The shield is then offset in the opposite direction; the line runs through the opposite hip.

3. The shield is moved off the ball and chest high; the line comes off under control and blocks linebackers aligned nose up by making contact at the armpit and running through the target. The procedure is repeated to the opposite armpit.

4. The shield is again off the ball and chest high, but now offset. The line comes off under control, making contact and running through the opposite armpit. The shield is again held chest high and off the ball but offset in the opposite direction. The block is executed in the opposite direction.

5. The shield holders move back to head up, still off the ball with the shield held chest high. On the starting count they move laterally. The blockers lead the backers to make contact, simulating a block on a linebacker reacting to flow. The shields are again moved to a head up linebacker position, with flow to the opposite direction and the lead by the blockers in the opposite direction.

6. The shield is moved up on the ball and into the gap; the shield holder drives through the gap. As explained previously, our target for the seal block or down block is the opposite hip. The block is executed in that manner by the offensive line. The shields are then moved to the opposite gaps and down or seal blocks are performed in the other direction.

Points or emphasis for the shield drill:

1. An offensive starting count is used.

2. Stress concentration by the blocker. He must be certain of the starting count, which foot to step with (mentally shifting his weight to the opposite foot), the proper target, and his footwork.

3. Resistance is offered with the shields.

4. Proper splits and alignment with relation to the ball is imperative.

Corrections can be made on the spot if they do not interfere with the tempo of the drill. The shield drill can be accomplished in about four or five minutes. It is done every day in the pre-season and twice weekly during the season. If personnel permits, junior varsity and varsity lines may be separated for the shield drill.

Pass Protection Drills

Passive pass protection is as different from blocking for the run as night is from day. The techniques and concept of one phase is completely foreign to the other. Under individual line play, it was explained that pass protection depends on (1) proper position of the body between the defender and the passer, (2) separation between the blocker and the defender, and (3) proper assignment. When the protection breaks down it may be traced to the preceding reasons.

At one time we only worked on pass protection in the individual drill and in full dummy or team scrimmages. We found that such a routine did not get the job done because we did not get nearly enough work and emphasis on the front line working together to protect the passer. Hence, we began including pass protection in offensive group work.

Pass protection is practiced with centers, guards, and tackles aligning on the ball, splitting, and assuming stances properly. The coach uses an offensive snap count and receives the ball from center. He retreats to a spot that is designated for the passer. A second group is armed with shields and attempts to get to the passer. Initially, all shield holders align close to the ball and simulate linemen by holding the shields low (Diagram 5-3).

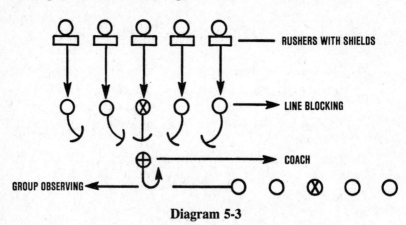

Diagram 5-3

Shield Pass Protection, Blocking Linemen

After two shots against rushing linemen for each group, defensive alignments are assumed by shield holders and blitzing and twisting stratagems may be utilized by the defenders (Diagram 5-4).

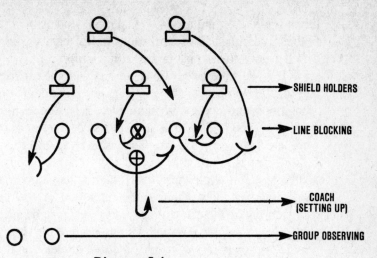

Diagram 5-4

Pass Protection, Blocking Rushing Alignments

The pass protection drill is executed at nearly all offensive practices during the pre-season and once each week during the season. The rushing patterns of the opponents are used in game weeks. This drill is usually run live for about four or five plays for each unit. I feel that a greater proportion of live work is called for in practicing pass blocking than in blocking the run. The pass rusher has more opportunity to use his hands; thus the use of the shield is not as realistic as it is for the run.

Teams that use full sprint-outs or action passes that involve aggressive pass blocking should employ these patterns as a part of the offensive line work period. Evaluations of the pass rush drill are made by occasionally videotaping the drill, enabling the coaches to screen it after practice. Otherwise, mistakes in individual execution can be made on the spot. About four to seven minutes is a good length of time for the drill.

Play Work

This is actually an offensive dummy scrimmage for the line. It is used to supplement the full team dummy scrimmage. I thoroughly cover the desired outcomes of a full dummy scrimmage later, but this drill is used because there are times that the offensive line needs more dummy work than the practice schedule allows for full team work. In such instances, the coaches can afford to take a little more time to refine techniques and polish assignments than they would in full team sessions, since corrections in full team work must be made "on the run" to simulate a game-like tempo.

The plays are called from the line with the offense positioning and splitting properly. This is a good learning device for defensive recognition and communication. Necessary blocking calls can be stressed for the line. A standard defense can be used for pre-season work and the expected defenses are worked against each week of the season. This is a particularly good drill for teaching blocking against a stunting defensive pattern. The stunt patterns are drawn on cards and a manager shows them to the shield holders before the play is run. Once again the effectiveness of the drill can be evaluated on the spot. It is good to do it live about one-third of the time. Four or five minutes is generally sufficient time to complete the drill (Diagram 5-5).

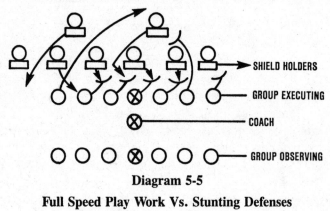

Diagram 5-5
Full Speed Play Work Vs. Stunting Defenses

DEVELOPING RUNNING BACKS THROUGH GROUP WORK

Teaching Running Plays

Timing, timing, timing! Regardless of the offense, backfield play is predicated on timing. The backs must work the plays again and again. The backfields are organized in three groups with a center assigned to each unit. The ball is placed on the hash mark and towels, cones, or other markers may be used as reference points on the line of scrimmage. A strip of plastic or rubber with the various spacings marked may also be used for each unit. The first and second groups work back to back with the third group crossfield (Diagram 5-6).

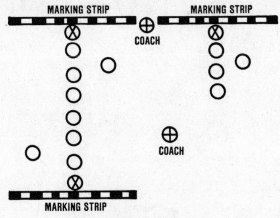

Diagram 5-6

Backs-Running Play Work

With this setup, two or three coaches can do an adequate job of teaching offensive plays. Correct alignment, stances, routes, and ball handling can be evaluated on the spot. Because of in-season time limitations, the drill is run only in the pre-season when it is used in each offensive session. It can be effective in time periods of seven to ten minutes. Defenders with shields may be added to incorporate blocking techniques.

Teaching Pass Offense with a Single Side Skeleton

It is a must that the passing game be timed adequately. During game weeks, we take a ten minute period once each week and work our passing game to a single side, splitting the period so that the ends on the opposite side work with the rest of the line while the other side ends and backs work the pass drill (Diagram 5-7).

Good preparation is essential for this drill. The coach should

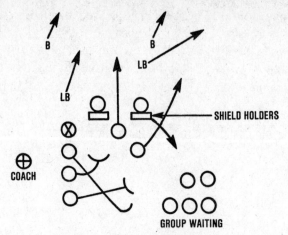

Diagram 5-7

Single Side Skeleton Pass Offense

decide what personnel will be used on defense and in what positions they will participate; this must be taken care of *before* going on the field. This information can be noted on a 4″ x 6″ note card so that the names and positions can be read rapidly at the beginning of the drill (Diagram 5-8).

S WILLIAMS

H DONCHEZ

CASCIOLA   KAISER
LB   LB

JONES   BEHAGEN
(SHIELD)   (SHIELD)

Diagram 5-8

Defensive Personnel Vs. Single Side Pass

On the flip side of the card, the plays to be run are listed. We do not diagram the plays, as we want our personnel to execute them as called. First and second units alternate the plays with a single center. The coach or a manager can read off the plays to the quarterback (Diagram 5-9).

Formation	Set-Up	Pattern
[1]I North	65 Pass	TE Out
[2]I North	65 Pass	TE Flag
[3]I North	65 Pass	TE Cross
[4]I Gee	Roll Odd	TE Cross
[5]I Gee	Roll Odd	Z Curl
[6]I North	Roll Odd	Wing Cross
[7]I Star	Roll Even	SE Out
[8]I Star	Sprint Even	————
[9]I Pro	Roll Even	SE Flag
[10]I Pro-Split	Roll Even	SE Cross
[11]I Pro-Split	Hitch	Hitch
[12]Star	Roll Even	SE Flag
[13]I Star	Roll Even	Slot Cross

Diagram 5-9: Single side skeleton pass plays

A lined and hashed field is a must for the drill. Blockers and rushers are added, but the rushers are generally using shields. The drill can be evaluated on the spot and is occasionally recorded. It is important to have managers spotting footballs so the plays can be run quickly.

Pass Offense—Two-Side Skeleton

This phase is executed in almost every offensive session during the pre-season and once each week during the season. Personnel must be listed to assume linebacker and deep back positions. Defensive rush positions, usually with shields, are also assigned. All personnel selection is done before going on the field. Names can be read rapidly at the beginning of the drill, with the defenders donning scrimmage vests or hats (Diagram 5-10).

Two groups may alternate and use a single center. If numbers allow, a third group may be assigned to take a third play for each of the other two groups. Managers must spot the ball quickly on a lined off field. The plays are listed by the coach on a note card prior to practice, so they can be passed on by the coach or a manager to the quarterbacks (Diagram 5-11). This should expedite the procedure. It is a good idea to occasionally record the drill on film or videotape from behind the offense. The drill consumes about fifteen minutes.

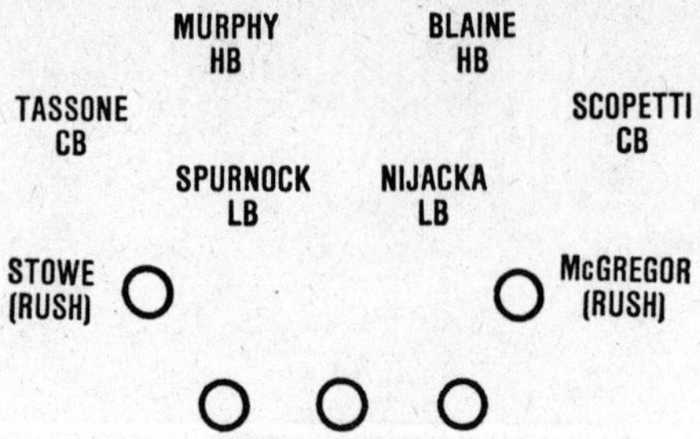

MURPHY
HB

BLAINE
HB

TASSONE
CB

SCOPETTI
CB

SPURNOCK
LB

NIJACKA
LB

STOWE
(RUSH)

McGREGOR
(RUSH)

Diagram 5-10

Defensive Personnel Vs. Pass Skeleton

Formation	Set-Up	Pattern
[1]I North	70 Screen Odd	———
[2]I Gee	70 Pass	———
[3]B North	Sprint Odd	———
[4]I Right	65 Pass	TE Only
[5]I Con-Split	65 Pass	TE Flag/Out
[6]I Haw-Split	65 Pass	Z Check
[7]I Sprint Even	Sprint Even	———
[8]I Pro	Roll Even	SE Flag
[9]I Pro-Split	Roll Even	Z Cross
[10]I Left	65 Pass	———
[11]I Port	65 Pass	———
[12]I Con	65 Pass	TE Out

Diagram 5-11: Pass Skeleton—Plays

SIX

Developing the Offense with Full Team Work

Full teamwork represents the last plateau on the progression of offensive football practice. This is the stage at which all the parts fit together to become a smooth functioning team. With correct emphasis on full teamwork, the offense will become properly timed.

DUMMY SCRIMMAGE

If your dummy scrimmages are carried out the way mine once were, you are wasting a lot of golden coaching time. My original concept of dummy scrimmage was to bring the squad together and run the whole thing "on the wing," calling whatever plays popped into my head, changing the defensive arrangement when I felt the need arose, and running the same play time after time until we achieved perfection. We often spent forty-five minutes to an hour on the drill and got little done.

Analyze what you want to accomplish with your dummy scrimmage. A good one will benefit the offense by: (1) going through the mechanics of the play-calling procedure, including the huddle and the call itself, making each team member responsible for translating the instructions into the mental process necessary to execute the assignment; (2) aligning the offense with proper splits, formation, and onside alignment; (3) causing the players to carry out the assignments for the called play; (4) requiring the proper technique be used for every maneuver; and (5) establishing a game-like tempo.

We have a dummy scrimmage every evening during the pre-season period and twice each week during the season. In order to maintain concentration, we allot twenty-four to thirty minutes for dummy work. We have found that more than thirty minutes is not beneficial.

Best results can be expected only if the dummy scrimmage is carefully planned. Good planning serves a twofold purpose; it tends to minimize wasted time, and also establishes a game-like tempo. We begin by assigning a squad of players to fill the positions of the "dummy" defense (Diagram 6-1). We post the dummy list on the bulletin board before practice, since we do not wish to waste time making selections on the field. We prepare a dummy sheet which lists the plays to be run (Diagram 6-2). In the pre-season, the dummy sheet is made up on the basis of the plays to be taught and to be reviewed in each particular session against the kinds of defenses desired. In-season, we prepare an offensive game plan and practice the desired plays against anticipated opponent defenses. The plan is made up on the basis of scouting reports and opponent films (Diagram 6-3). A great deal of thought can be put into the formulation of the dummy sheet as to frequency of plays, personnel, formation, blocking assignments, variations, and so on. You must decide how the limited number of plays you will run can best be practiced (Diagram 6-4).

Anticipated defenses are drawn up on construction paper and numbered in sequence according to the dummy sheet. Stunts or slants can be indicated on the cards by using a different color marker to indicate the stunt routes (Diagram 6-5).

The dummy scrimmage is organized so that all the defenders are holding shields. A manager is assigned to spot the ball in a predetermined spot after each play. Another manager has the dummy sheet, reads the play to each quarterback, and checks it off with a pencil. The offense is organized into two units with some spares who alternate with the second unit. The huddles are designated by cone markers. As soon as the manager gives the play to the quarterback, he repeats it to the team and the squad advances to the

Sludgestickers

LE—Gdovic
LT—Foster
N—Murphy
RT—Oravitz
RE—Means
LLB—Simmons
RLB—Godet
M—Williams
LH—Pearson
S—Vinson
RH—Vupich

Diagram 6-1: Position List for Dummy Defense

Formation	Play		Defense
I North	65		#1
I Right	65		#1
I Star	65		#1
I Star	64		#1
I North	64		#1
I Right	64		#1
Quick Right	65		#1
Quick Right	64		#1
East	65		#1
West	65		#1
I Gee	64		#1
I Pro	65		#1
I North	65		#2
I Star	64		#2
I North-East	65		#2
I South-West	65		#2
I Star	64		#2
I North	65 Pass-TE Out		#2
I North	65 Pass-TE Flg		#2
I North	65 Pass-W Cr		#1
I Right	65 Pass-TE-H		#1
East	65 Pass-TE-H		#1
I North-East	65 Pass-TE-H		#1
I Gee	65 Pass-TE Out		#1
I Pro	65 Pass		#1

Diagram 6-2: Dummy Sheet for Pre-Season Practice

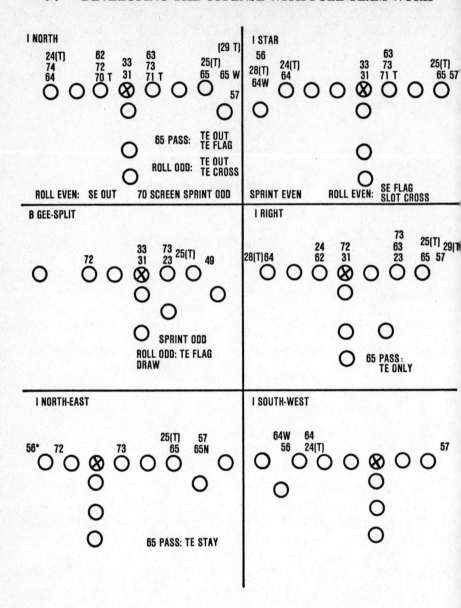

Diagram 6-3

Offensive Game Plan

Formation	*Play*		*Defense*
I North	25	#1	
I North	29	#1	
I North	65	#1	
I North	65 Wide	#1	
I North	65 Pass TE Out	#2	
I North	65 Pass TE Flag	#2	
I North	70 Screen Odd	#2	
I North	24	#2	
I North	63	#1	
I North	62	#1	
I North	57	#1	
I North	70 Trap	#1	
I North	71 Trap	#1	
I Star	70 Trap	#3	
I Star	71 Trap	#3	
I Star	64 Wide	#2	
I Star	33	#2	
I Star	73	#3	
I Star	72	#3	
I Star	56	#3	
I Star	Roll Even SE Flag	#4	
I Star	Roll Even Slot Cross	#4	
I Star	28	#4	
B Gee-Split	Sprint Odd	#4	
I North-East	56	#2	

Diagram 6-4: Dummy Sheet for In-Season Practice

line of scrimmage and runs the play. A third manager has the defensive cards and shows the proper card to the defense at the time the manager with the dummy sheet alerts him to do so.

We run two units and try to correct the mistakes in each one, but we do not want to break our tempo by giving a "clinic" on the field. We want corrections to be made by the position coach on the move. The objective is to run the plays properly but to get through them in the alloted time, making good concentration and great physical effort imperative. Videotape or film of the dummy scrimmage is taken from behind the offense, with a frame width from end to end. It is an invaluable aid (Diagram 6-6). By using the dummy

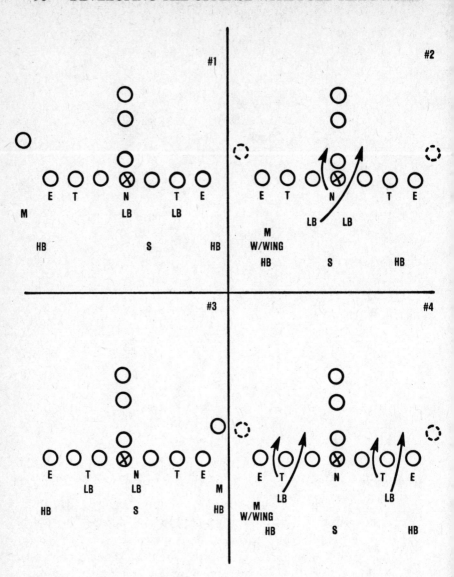

Diagram 6-5

Opponent Defenses on Cards

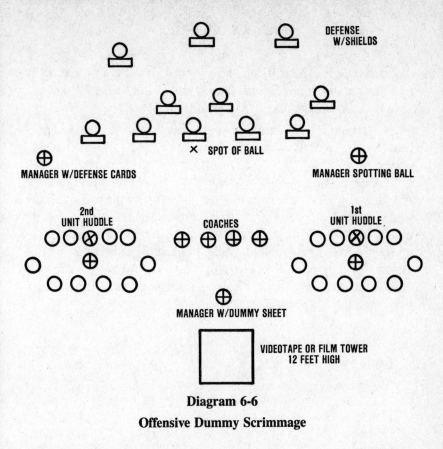

Diagram 6-6

Offensive Dummy Scrimmage

sheet, each assignment and technique can be thoroughly checked for all the plays. We seldom show the dummy scrimmage film to the players but serious assignment or technique errors can be corrected prior to practice the next day by having each position coach make notes, and conferring with the player while dressing for practice the following afternoon.

We occasionally stop a play and repeat it during dummy scrimmage, but we generally refrain from doing this, as the officials do not give us this opportunity on the game field. Our emphasis is to get each play the best we can every time we run it and improvement in execution will come. We believe that too many repetitions of a poorly executed play would break down our method of organization.

BREAKAWAY DRILLS

The only effective way I have found to coach backs to run in the open field is to actually put them in traffic and have them run. As a result, we developed the breakaway drill, which also allows us a little live scrimmage and some over-the-field work.

After dummy scrimmages in pre-season practice, we generally run about three or four minutes of breakaway drills. We use the drill once a week during the season, but the time period is about sixteen or seventeen minutes. We have the dummy defense put aside their shields and go live. A manager spots the ball and the coach has the first unit run four or five plays in our pre-season phase. The second unit comes in and run about two plays. We run against reserve personnel so that our running backs frequently get into the secondary and learn to run in an open field. We also get work in moving the offense around in various field positions, spotting the ball and huddling.

Formation	Play		Defense
I North	63 Double	#4	
I Star	75 Counter	#6	
I Pro	Roll Even SE Flag	#6	
B North	49	#6	(Gerhart)
I Right	57	#3	(Mulligan)
I Star	56	#3	
I Star	Sprint Even	#3	(Wise)
I North	65 Pass TE Out	#7	
I North	74 Counter	#7	(Dogget)
A Star	22	#4	
B Gee	23 Pass	#7	(Mulligan)
I North	31 Wedge	#7	
B Star	33 Trap	#9	
I Gee	70 Pass	#6	(Scott)
East	23	#6	
I North	65	#4	
I North	65 Wide	#4	

Diagram 6-7: Ready List for Breakaways

During the season, a dummy personnel list is posted to determine the players to be used in the role of the defensive "scout" squad against breakaways. Most of the time we establish a scout squad at the beginning of the practice week and maintain it throughout the week, since this lends consistency in execution of alignments, stunts, and coverages. Prepare a 4″ x 6″ index card which includes the play and the defense you wish to see against each play (Diagram 6-7). Indicate to the quarterback the play and at the same time tell a manager which defense to show the defensive unit. The card also indicates which substitutions you wish to make in certain play-calling situations. We substitute individually in this period. This is usually all the offensive scrimmaging that we do during the season.

A variation of the drill is to make the defensive front live without tackling and have only the secondary members tackle. It is good to use better personnel as defenders in this drill and you get the same effect by "breaking" the runner into the open, except it is a little tougher to block the defense up front and the secondary defenders are better tacklers.

BEAT THE CLOCK DRILLS

The waning moments of a game or half often decide the contest. A team must be well drilled in order to conserve time and run off as many well-executed plays as possible. The first step in preparing a team to best use these precious minutes is to teach each player the rules for starting and stopping the clock. Any player may call time out but we discipline our players to call time out only when the coach signals to do so.

The squad should be impressed that it is possible to conserve time by going out of bounds, running more than a single play from the same huddle, calling plays from the line of scrimmage, or lining up on the ball and throwing a quick sideline pass that will stop the clock (since it will be out of bounds even if completed).

During the pre-season, we scrimmage the beat-the-clock drill once for a period of twenty minutes. We go against third string personnel. Two coaches act as officials, while the rest of the coaches and non-players are on the sideline just as in a game. The defenders are instructed to attempt to keep the ball carrier on the ground when the clock is running so the offense will actually have to fight to get off the pile and get back to the huddle or to the line. One of the coach-officials keeps track of the time with a stopwatch and the head coach administers the play-calling, substitutions, time-outs, and strategy from the sideline. Once the season is underway, the drill is carried out the day before the game against no defense. Situations are called out by the assistant coaches, so the squad gets an opportunity to work on saving those valuable seconds while marching up the field. We feel that this enables us to get in just enough offense on the day prior to the game to maintain our timing, as we do no other offensive team work that particular day.

OVER THE FIELD SERIES

We practice an over-the-field series occasionally in the preseason practice. We work against shields. The drill is organized and run in much the same way we run the breakaway drills, with the coach listing the plays to be used against the desired defenses. The drill approximates a dummy scrimmage up and down the field, using various hash and down and distance situations. About fourteen or fifteen plays are run by a unit; then we go to a second unit and run about ten plays. We run this drill for about twenty minutes.

SITUATION DRILLS

If we completely platooned offensive personnel, we would do some of this each week, but time does not permit us to use this variation of dummy scrimmage very often. The drill is organized so that all third and short plays are practiced for a period by using the offensive game plan for that situation against the anticipated defenses (Diagram 6-8). It is set up with a dummy sheet and practiced just as in the dummy scrimmage drill. The same is done for second and long, third and long, second and short, fourth and short or fourth and long in four down territory, inside the offense's own ten, or inside the opponent's ten. The drill offers most of the advantages of the conventional dummy scrimmage in addition to lending emphasis to each particular phase of the offensive game plan.

We run a short period against anticipated goal line defense of

Third and Short—Three Down Territory

Formation	Play	Defense
I North	65	#10
I North	64	#10
I North	65 Pass	#10
I North	31 Wedge	#10
I star	64	#11
I Star	64 Keep	#11
I Star	65	#11

Diagram 6-8: Situation Drill Dummy Sheet

each opponent each week. It is our philosophy to use the same plays on the goal line that have been successful for us over the field, but we must get in some work with the restricted field and against goal line defenses.

LOW INTENSITY DUMMY SCRIMMAGE

We do this *once* a year. The drill lasts about forty-five minutes and we schedule it as a separate practice session midday on Wednesday on the second week of two-a-day sessions. This is where we break our rules on intensity and tempo. We have installed most of our offense by this time and we regard this as a "blackboard-on-the-field" session. We still use the dummy sheet and defensive cards, but we stop the drill and work through assignments quite often. The drill is an excellent change of pace and straightens out a lot of assignments.

SEVEN

Coaching Defensive Ends with Game-Tested Drills

A good defensive end has the physical characteristics of a good linebacker, although in our scheme he does not get involved in pass coverage. We teach two basic kinds of end play: (1) a wide or outside kind of play, and (2) a position on an offensive man so that the end is reading the opponent and reacting to his block. We can supplement the basic play with alignment and charge modifications.

AGILITY DRILLS

Agility drills teach and promote body control, a necessity in good fundamental play. We do agility drills at every morning practice in the pre-season and once each week during the season. We also use a lot of agility drills in the summer conditioning program. The drills are carefully taught and the players must understand that they are not races; correct form is imperative. When form is achieved, speed will follow. Three repetitions of each drill are run. We like to have four or less in each group for each action, so we try to break the personnel into three groups. The drills used are as follows:

1. *Carioca*—This is a fine footwork drill and it also tends to make the hips more flexible. The coach faces the first group about ten yards away from the players. The players are on a marked line about four yards apart with hips low, weight on the balls of their feet. The coach signals with right or left arm, and the players execute the carioca in the direction of the arm signal. The carioca is executed by putting one foot beyond the other and in front of the other foot, then moving the other foot in the same direction. The starting foot is then placed beyond but behind the other foot, then moving that foot in the same direction. The players go hard for ten yards and then return to the end of the line.

2. *Shuffle wave drill*—This is an excellent change of direction drill. The initial set-up is the same as for the carioca. The coach gives a signal for the players to come forward by dropping a hand. The players sprint forward and the coach quickly gives a hand signal to either side. On recognition, the players plant their lead foot on the side they are moving, then reverse direction, shuffling to the side of the signal, keeping the hips down and shoulders parallel. The coach quickly indicates another direction change which causes the players to plant their lead foot and reverse direction again. The coach never gives more than three reactions in the drill and frequently gives only two reactions. More than three reactions makes the drill a conditioning drill, not an agility drill, which tends to make the players pace themselves. The coach must be alert to encourage the players not to anticipate a change in direction or to zig-zag and gain ground during direction changes. The coach concludes the drill by yelling "Go," which signals the players to sprint past the coach. There are three repetitions of the drill.

3. *Lateral snake drill*—The ends align single file and shuffle over the snake, a high-stepping device that is tubular with rods protruding from it. The ends make one trip down and one trip back. The snake shuffle provides good footwork practice and teaches the defenders to pick up the feet to step over the "trash" at the same time.

4. *Mirror shuffle*—The players are set up in groups of two, one acting as a runner, the other acting as a shuffler. Six cylindrical dummies are spaced five yards apart. The runner jogs in a direction that will take the shuffler over the

cylinder dummies, moving with shoulders parallel, remaining about one yard behind the ball carrier. The jogger can reverse direction once or twice at any point in his route, forcing the shuffler to do the same and remain shuffling. The jogger also changes speeds. Each shuffler gets one turn from each side (Diagram 7-1).

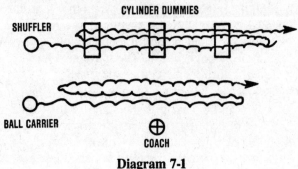

Diagram 7-1

Mirror Shuffle Drill

STANCE

Good defensive stance is more important for ends than any other defensive position. Poor stances contribute to poor reaction and defensive shedding positions, and *position* is the ultimate in defensive play.

After the agility period, on the first day of practice we align the defensive ends in rows of three and teach the defensive stance. We repeat the stance drill the second practice and do not teach the stance separately after the second day. The stance will be a checkpoint for the coach in administering all other drills.

We emphasize a stance with feet about shoulder width apart and even. We want the hips depressed and the arms hanging loosely. We overcoach the low stance as we feel this is a good starting point in keeping the end low in meeting offensive blockers.

FORM TACKLING

This is a vital defensive fundamental. Poor tackling will cost you time after time. You can teach this fundamental and keep the players sharp without turning your practices into armed combat zones, resulting in too much hitting and lots of injuries.

We teach tackling at very slow speeds. With one exception, we do no live tackling in the fundamental period. We feel that we will get enough "live" work with our defensive scrimmage periods during the week.

Tackling is taught by having each end face a partner across a marked line. The groups must be separated by at least four yards. On command, one of the lines runs at the opponent and makes contact, while the other line takes its turn and does the same. The tacklers are to assume the hitting position with hips down and feet about shoulder width apart. They focus their eyes on the numerals of the opponent and run through that target. We emphasize chest on chest and do not teach an extension. It is very simply a run *through* the ball carrier. With this approach, we believe we have reduced the problem of overextension and missing the ball carrier. With daily repetition of the drill, the tackler will learn to deliver a blow on contact as a natural progression of the technique. If the extension and the blow is emphasized, we feel that it will cause problems in overextension. We have each player form tackle four times in each drill.

Next, we have the tacklers run through the target but *club* the arms in back of the thighs on contact. The ball carriers are stationary and passive, allowing themselves to be driven back easily. Three repetitions are used for each line.

During all pre-season defensive workouts we work on making angle tackles, by have the ball carrier run slowly at an angle as the tackler runs through the target and clubs the arms. Each player gets one angle tackle in each direction. We do not use the drill once the season has begun.

A tackling drill used for every defensive session is the skate drill, where the defender shuffles behind the ball carrier, meeting him square on the line as he turns up. We only make contact on this drill and do not take the ball carrier down (Diagram 7-2). Each player gets one shot in each direction.

The full contact tackling drill that we use is only done once each season. We utilize it in order to get the players ready for full scale scrimmage so it is done the first day we schedule a full scale

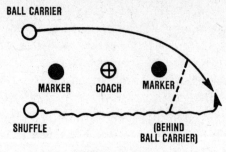

Diagram 7-2

Skate Drill

scrimmage, usually the third day of practice (the scrimmage will last about twenty minutes). The drill is valuable because it gets us ready to tackle from all kinds of body positions and angles. Two markers are spaced three yards apart and a ball is placed on the ground. The tackler is on his back and the ball carrier is facing the opposite direction. Both are spaced two yards from the ball. On the coach's signal, the ball carrier turns, picks up the ball and runs, while the tackler gets to his feet and executes the tackle. The coach stops action with a whistle, being alert for the twisting of ankles or possible predicaments that could lead to injuries. These can usually be avoided with a quick whistle.

TEACHING DEFENSIVE TECHNIQUE

In teaching defensive technique, we categorize the teaching progression into a four-step process:

1. The first teaching step is the description of the overall technique. We describe the technique in detail on the blackboard before taking the field for the first teaching session. On the field, after the stretching, agility, and form tackling, we explain in careful detail the particular technique to be taught, review it a bit more quickly the second day, more quickly yet on the third day, after which it is unnecessary to go through the explanation of the entire technique.
2. The next step entails the alignment and initial key and charge or reaction. We drill this phase carefully the first day

it is taught for each technique, then go over it quickly each day after that in the pre-season. We drill for this phase during the season once each week in weeks we will use the particular technique in the game.

3. Next, we teach the defenders to shed blocks. We do this every time we practice defense.

4. Last, we go through the proper pursuit pattern for each given technique. We drill this every time we work on defense in the pre-season, and once each week during the season when we will employ the technique in the game that week.

LOOSE TECHNIQUE

The Loose technique is the wide end play. Our end aligns three feet outside the tight end as close to the line of scrimmage as he can. He keys the near back, and makes a quick two-step charge at a slight angle inside. If the key should dive or come to him, he alerts for a block, meeting it with great force by stepping into it with the inside

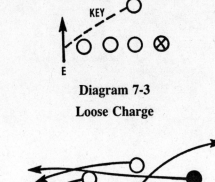

Diagram 7-3

Loose Charge

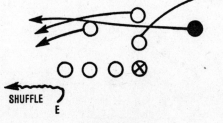

Diagram 7-4

Forcing Wide Play to Sideline

forearm on the inside shoulder of the blocker. The defender is to keep his shoulders parallel to the line of scrimmage and remain on the line of scrimmage (Diagram 7-3). The concept of the Loose technique is to be able to close the inside play and to shuffle outside with the shoulders square in order to force the wide play to the sideline (Diagram 7-4). The defender must not allow a blocker to get to his feet; he protects himself from the "chop" block by getting his hands down to deflect the blocker and springing his legs back slightly. On the option, the loose end will initially be taught to defend against the pitch. He does this by remaining static after his charge, waiting for the quarterback to close him, then taking a quick jab step to the quarterback, and chasing the pitch to the outside if it is made (Diagram 7-5). Plays developing inside the end are closed by shuffling inside the end with shoulders square, then turning and pursuing when certain the play will not break outside. Plays developing to the other side will alert the end to remain static for the long counter (which he would close as any other power play) (Diagram 7-6), the bootleg (which he must penetrate and force on

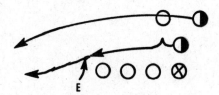

Diagram 7-5

Playing the Option

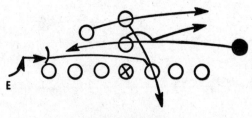

Diagram 7-6

Playing the Long Counter

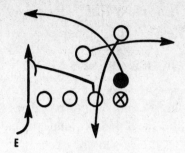

Diagram 7-7

Defending the Bootleg

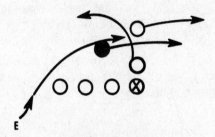

Diagram 7-8

Deep Reverse Leverage

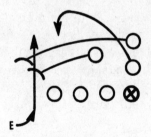

Diagram 7-9

Pass Rush

the passer's inside shoulder) (Diagram 7-7), and the ball to the other side (which will mean deep reverse leverage, positioning on the back shoulder of the deepest back, and trailing until the reverse threat is no longer authentic, at which point he assumes a pursuit angle) (Diagram 7-8). Drop back and action passes to the end's side will be closed by a penetrating rush to the passer's inside shoulder (Diagram 7-9).

LOOSE CHARGE DRILL

We use the loose charge drill every day in the pre-season but eliminate it during the season, since it is a part of every defensive play. If we are having a great deal of trouble making the charge, we may go back to it during the season.

All the ends can do the charge simultaneously and the setup is the same as for the stance drill. The charge for loose involves two very quick short steps, moving the outside foot, then the inside foot, directing at a very slight angle to the inside. We emphasize that the defender remain very low throughout the charge by keeping the hips down. (The inexperienced player will tend to elevate his hips at the beginning of the charge.) Since all ends must prepare to play on both sides, we take four charges from the right end position and four from the left end position. There is a reversal of the foot action when changing sides.

KEYING AND REACTING—LOOSE TECHNIQUE

We set up cones and use a near back, quarterback, and fullback. We draw up moves for the offense on cards, and have our end make his charge and react to the different plays the end must react to. We include the sweep, kick out, option, drop back, action pass, bootleg, and action away (Diagram 7-10). We use this drill without any contact the first three days of pre-season, put contact in for the second part of the drill on the second and third days, and always combine the entire drill with contact the rest of the pre-

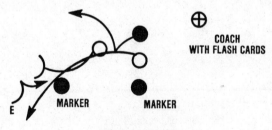

Diagram 7-10
Keying and Reacting-Loose

season. During the season, we combine the drill with contact once each week and tailor the offensive moves to conform to those of the team we are playing. We draw the offensive moves up on play cards.

SHEDDING THE BLOCK

I think you must isolate this phase of defensive play and work on it every day in the individual period when you practice defense. Although shedding is combined in the keying and reacting drills, most all semi-group, group, and team defensive drills, it is a fundamental that must be worked and worked and worked. We align the ends in groups of three and have partners with shields coming from a route marked with cones. The ends stay very low and when the shield closes, step into the inside part of the shield with a hard forearm extension with the right forearm into the lower numerals of the defender, stepping simultaneously with the right foot. The idea is to neutralize the blocker, then to push him away with the hands, keeping the shoulders square. Each defender gets three shots from each direction. The third day of pre-season practice we must incorporate the low block into the action, and continue its use every time we drill individual defense. We have the blockers come out and attack the outside knee of the defenders. The ends are responsible for getting their hands on the blockers and keeping their legs free. Each defender gets two shots from each side.

SQUEEZE TECHNIQUE

We introduce this technique the third day of pre-season practice and work on it every day the rest of the summer sessions and once each week during the season, if we have the technique in the game plan that week. In this alignment the feet are one yard off the tight end's hands, with the inside foot splitting the stance (we can modify the depth and shade of the alignment). The defender keys the tight end and matches his feet. If the blocker steps with the inside foot, our defender mirrors and steps with the corresponding foot in the same direction. The defender protects himself from the block of the tight end by extending a two-hand, open-handed uppercut under the shoulder pads of the blocker. If the blocker drives at our defender, the mirrored footstep and uppercut neutralizes the blocker, enabling the defender to push him out of the way and pick up the flow of the backs. If the blocker is blocking down, the defender moves to the inside and keeps the shoulders square, alerting for another block from inside out; he should make it very difficult for the end to release inside. If the end releases outside, the defender shuffles out and remains in a low position, looking for another block or secondary reaction. All secondary reactions are the same as for the Loose technique. The kick-out, sweep, passes, and flow away reactions will be no different from the reactions previously taught in Loose technique (Diagram 7-11).

Diagram 7-11

Squeeze Reactions

UPPERCUT DRILL—SQUEEZE TECHNIQUE

The uppercut must be a powerful blow or your defender will be driven way off the ball. We line up seven defenders on the pads of a seven-man sled and have them step with the right foot and simultaneously deliver a two-hand uppercut on a signal from the coach, quickly bringing the other foot up to a parallel position. Six uppercuts stepping with the right foot and six stepping with the left foot will accomplish the purpose of the drill. We use this drill every time we drill the Squeeze technique. Regardless of how well-schooled your defender is in keying and pursuit, if he cannot deliver a blow, he will not be a good defender. You must teach and drill effective block protection; it is even more important for a reading technique such as the Squeeze.

INITIAL ALIGNMENT, KEY, AND REACTION—SQUEEZE TECHNIQUE

We align four defenders across from four blockers with shields. The coach faces the offense and gives hand signals for the blocker's maneuver. The end will deliver his uppercut and react initially to the moves of the dummy tight end (Diagram 7-12). We use this drill every time we work on the Squeeze and about half the time we discard the shields and have the blockers come out live.

SHIELD HOLDERS STEPPING ACCORDING TO COACH'S SIGNALS

DEFENDERS DELIVERING UPPERCUT AND MIRRORING STEP OF BLOCKER

⊕ COACH

Diagram 7-12

Key and Reaction—Squeeze Technique

FULL REACTION—SQUEEZE TECHNIQUE

The set up is with a tight end, two running backs, and a quarterback. Play cards are used and the end plays Squeeze reactions and responds to the flow of the backs after the initial key. Every end gets a couple of shots to each side (Diagram 7-13). We do this every day after the introduction of the Squeeze in the pre-season and usually once a week during the season, with the offensive patterns tailored to conform to those of our opponents.

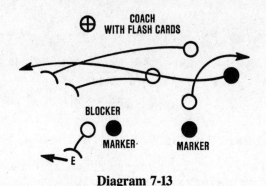

⊕ COACH
WITH FLASH CARDS

BLOCKER

MARKER·   MARKER

E

Diagram 7-13

Full Reaction—Squeeze Technique

CRASH TECHNIQUE

We can execute the Crash from any alignment. The object of the Crash technique is to drive to a point one yard behind the hips of the offensive tackle's alignment, jamming all of the offensive traffic in the path. The end will have the quarterback on the option and someone else must be responsible to contain the sprint out pass and the sweep. All other reactions are as for the Loose or Squeeze. The Crash is best employed as a surprise maneuver and serves as a good changeup for the other techniques.

CRASH CHARGE DRILL

We place six markers as the points for the charge directing the players on the proper route (Diagram 7-14). Four reps in each direction are carried out. We only do this drill on the day it is introduced. After we complete the initial teaching drill, we have our end run through an attacking shield man and always drill it that way for the rest of the pre-season and once in weeks when Crash is part of the game plan. We must emphasize to the players that the charge is made with reckless abandon. The tendency is to tiptoe through the charge cautiously, particularly after the emphasis on the flat style of play previously taught. We have found no way to teach the Crash other than to force the defender through the shield hard.

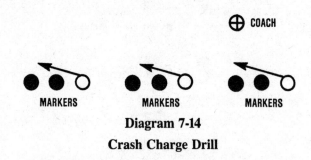

Diagram 7-14

Crash Charge Drill

FULL REACTION—CRASH TECHNIQUE

We set this up just as the Loose drill, and go through the plays so the defender can get his reactions. The drill is full-speed without tackling and we do it three times during the pre-season and once in weeks when we are going to Crash.

TECHNIQUE MODIFICATIONS

We may want a quick force in the backfield for certain reasons, or we may want to get deep if a sweep, pass, or option shows; we may want to change option assignments or the way we play the pitch—whatever modification we wish should not be too difficult. We install it in the game plan for a given week and drill it in the individual defensive period for that week.

PASS RUSH TECHNIQUE

Pass rush techniques are often overlooked on the secondary school level. The concept is to make a move and to keep accelerating the feet, a difficult habit to establish. You must spend a great deal of time teaching and drilling pass rush technique with the ends, particularly if you are emphasizing the flat style of play against the run. We teach the rush techniques on the fourth day of pre-season practice, and we work on rush techniques every other day in the pre-season and when necessary during the season. We introduce three rush techniques to the ends and have each end try all three techniques. In the second week, we ask the ends to each choose one or two rush techniques and concentrate on them in subsequent drills.

Ends are usually pass blocked by a back or a lineman dropping into the backfield. We begin the rush technique drill by having the coach walk each end through the technique on a heavy bag (Diagram 7-15).

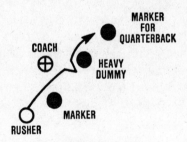

Diagram 7-15

Walk Through Pass Rush

The first method to be taught is the shoulder dip and spin. The end accelerates his feet and drives for the bag. He dips the outside shoulder and strikes the dummy in the middle with the outside shoulder by simultaneously stepping with the outside foot, pivoting on that foot after contact, and spinning around the bag (Diagram 7-16). Each player gets walked through from each side, then goes against a shield holder twice from each side on the first day of the

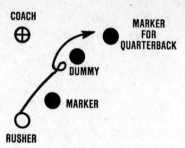

Diagram 7-16

Shoulder Dip and Spin Drill

drill. After that, we alternate some live work with the shield work. The important fundamental to emphasize in all pass rushing is to keep the feet moving.

The second pass rush maneuver for the end is the uppercut and shed. The end hits a shield with a two-hand open-hand uppercut, then pushes the opponent's elbow or arm and throws him aside, overcoming the theory of passive pass protection which is to keep the defender disengaged from the blocker and the blocker in the defender's pursuit line. This is done with a shield and each defender gets two shots for each side. The techniques *must* be executed with the feet moving.

The last rush technique is the head and shoulder fake. The defender must get close to the blocker by running directly for his middle, then suddenly shift his weight by taking a misdirection step; if the blocker shifts his weight to meet the anticipated new charge angle, the defender's next step should free him for the rush (the step after the initial misdirection step will take the defender to the other side of the blocker) (Diagram 7-17). After the rush techniques are introduced, we practice the rush drill every other day in the pre-season. Because of the demands of time, we work this drill only occasionally during the season.

A modified rush drill is used to give us some work against the move-out pass, where the blocker will be attacking the ends aggressively. The end must penetrate and shed the block with a forearm raise, just as he would shed the blocker for a running play, then attack the passer by running a line to the inside shoulder. We use a player to assume the position of quarterback for the drill and we do not tackle him, but rush with hands high. It is permissible to

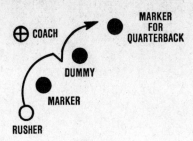

Diagram 7-17

Head and Shoulder Fake Pass Rush

jump to deflect the pass only if the front elbow of the passer drops as part of the passing motion. The backside end must rush the action passer by using a standard pass rush technique on the passive blocker, then positioning for the *back* shoulder of the quarterback and accelerating to the target. This position prevents the passer from reversing and deepening, thus escaping from containment. The hands need not be held high for the backside rush (Diagram 7-18). This phase of the drill is used twice in the pre-season and once in game weeks when we are preparing for the moveout pass. Group pass rush drills, defensive front drills, and defensive scrimmages provide enough additional repetition for us to adequately refine our pass rush against all kinds of passes.

Drill form tackling, block protection, and initial keying and reading every time you practice defensive end play. Use other drills according to the game plan and as a brush up.

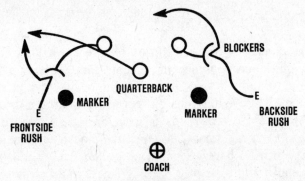

Diagram 7-18

Move Out Pass Rush Drill

EIGHT

Developing Down Linemen for Defense

Our theory is that defensive players who line up in a stance are to penetrate and reestablish a new line of scrimmage one yard behind the ball. Therefore, the priority is to penetrate the line of scrimmage and then to read and react to the block. The stance and drills for down linemen are all designed with the priority of penetration, then reaction.

AGILITY DRILLS

The objectives of agility drills for the down linemen are to practice quick reactions and movements and to get them used to hitting the ground. As a result, their agility work is not the same as that of the ends. We align the players so that four at a time do the agility drill. Three repetitions of each drill are carried out. The exception to our alignment and repetition procedure is the monkey roll, for which we have a separate procedure.

The all fours wave drill has the players in a four-point stance with the eyes focused on the coach who is about ten yards upfield. The coach drops his hand, which starts the players forward on all fours. The coach then points laterally and the players move in that direction on all fours. The coach then points in the opposite direction, which causes the players to go the opposite way. After no more than three direction changes, the coach will yell "Go," which signals the players to come up and sprint past the coach. To carry out the drill properly, the players must move laterally immediately on the signal. It is imperative that they not zigzag; sharp direction changes are a must. It is important that the players go at full speed during the entire maneuver. There is a tendency to anticipate the direction change by the coach (Diagram 8-1) and to slow up before the signal is actually given.

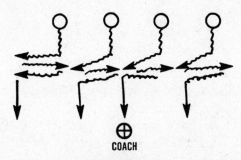

COACH

Diagram 8-1

All Fours Wave Drill

The seat roll starts with the players in four point stances. The coach signals a direction and the players pivot on the foot on the direction side and roll quickly on the buttocks back to the all fours position. The coach will give three directions and may change directions or use the same direction for consecutive signals if he wishes. After the three reactions, the coach will yell "go" and the players will come up and sprint past the coach, who was initially ten yards from the players.

The monkey roll is a tumbling drill. Players are arranged in groups of three with one player on his back, another adjacent on all fours, and another standing. The player on the ground takes a long body roll while the middle player springs over the top of the roller, then rolls under the standing player who springs over him, who rolls under the outside player. This sequence is repeated by the group until the whistle blows ending the drill. The coach lets the drill go about thirty seconds, insisting the players be quick in their movements. We have the players rest a few seconds, then blowing the whistle for another ten-second bout.

DEFENSIVE STANCES

If we are to get the defenders off with the rolling start, a good stance is essential. All the linemen are aligned on a marked line with the fingers on the line. The stance is similar to that of our offensive linemen except more weight is on the hands. The neck is bulled and the back is flat, with the buttocks at about the same elevation as the head. The heels are a little higher off the ground than in the offensive stance. The drill is used the first two days of pre-season practice and then eliminated, since stance is checked as a part of other drills.

DEFENSIVE STARTS

This is the cornerstone of our down lineman play. It is just as important for the penetrating defensive rushman to get a good start as it is for the offensive team.

The rushmen are in four-point stances and the coach holds a football, simulating a center on the line of scrimmage. The coach barks a cadence and moves the ball. We want the rusher to try and anticipate the snap and get a rolling start. If the rushman is moving just before or at the snap, he has gained a decided advantage. Early in the pre-season we do not concern ourselves too much with being offsides; this should come under control as the work progresses. We study the opponents each week so that we can get certain tips as to how they execute the starting count in order to gain an advantage in our defensive charge. We constantly emphasize the value of a rolling start. We allow the defenders to start with either foot. The drill is used in every individual defensive period.

GAP CHARGE

We want our gap charger to perform his move in such a way that it is difficult for either offensive linemen to block him to the inside. At the same time, we do not want to give away the inside as a result of being turned out or trapped.

We have the defender align his inside foot on the outside foot of the inside offensive lineman. We like to have some separation rather than be tight on the ball, so we instruct the rushman to put his hands eighteen inches off the ball. This enables him to get a slight rolling start and still be onside. The defender drives for the gap and wants to get a yard's penetration. If we can drill the start and coach good leg movement, we are well on the road to developing a good penetrating lineman. The refinement of the gap charge involves drilling the defender to read and react while on the move. In theory, the rushman will establish a new line of scrimmage one yard behind the ball and move along the new line. The rushman is drilled to key the initial moves of the offensive lineman to his inside. If the lineman blocks or pulls to the inside, the defender stops the charge and begins a move to the inside with his shoulders square (Diagram 8-2). Regardless of the key of the inside blocker, the rushman has a definite reaction pattern if the outside blocker comes down. When that happens, the rushman keeps accelerating unless the blocker has position on him (head across), which directs the rushman to brake his charge and cross the face of the blocker with shoulders parallel (Diagram 8-3).

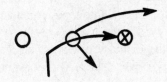

Diagram 8-2

Gap Charge—Inside Reaction

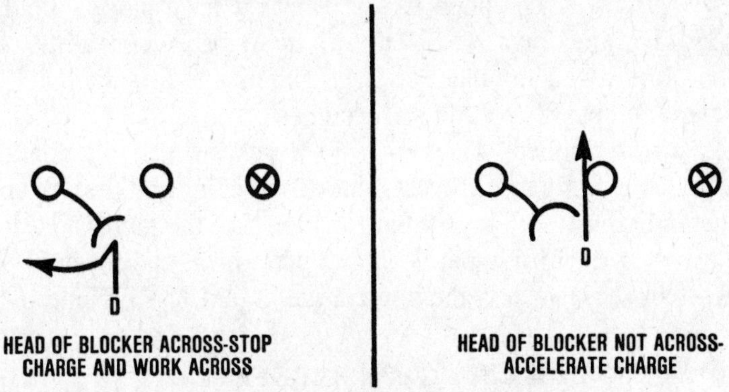

HEAD OF BLOCKER ACROSS-STOP
CHARGE AND WORK ACROSS

HEAD OF BLOCKER NOT ACROSS-
ACCELERATE CHARGE

Diagram 8-3

Gap Charge—Down Block

Diagram 8-4

Gap Charge—Hook Block Reaction

Diagram 8-5

Gap Charge—Turn Out Reaction

The rushman accelerates through the hook block by the inside lineman (Diagram 8-4), but stops and gets across the turn out block (Diagram 8-5). He accelerates into a pass rush when he recognizes a pass block. All the keyed reactions are secondary reactions and must be subordinated to the primary objective of penetration. The hard penetrating gap charger who can read on the move will play havoc with any offense.

GAP CHARGE THROUGH RESISTANCE DRILL

We align the defender in a stance and have players holding cylinder dummies just wide enough apart for the head to slip through. The coach simulates a starting count and lifts the ball. The defender attempts his rolling start, comes off level, and accelerates through the dummies. The points of emphasis are: (1) charging quickly, (2) charging with force, and (3) keeping the feet moving. The defender must strain very hard to penetrate the gap. The drill is used for every defensive period in the pre-season and for defensive practices in-season when the gap charge is part of the game plan.

DRILLING GAP CHARGES LIVE

You can not teach penetrating line play without frequently drilling the charge against live blockers. There is no substitute for this drill. The coach aligns the defender in a gap between two

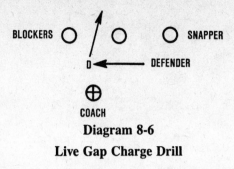

Diagram 8-6

Live Gap Charge Drill

offensive linemen. Another player is in a position to lift the ball (Diagram 8-6). The coach can signal the two blockers as to which blocking scheme to use and give them the starting count. Another player can lift the ball while the coach is barking the cadence. The defender gets his rolling start and reacts to the blocking patterns. We use this drill every day after the third day in the pre-season period and in-season in weeks in which we plan to utilize particular gap charges. It is possible to add a player to serve as a back to enable the defender to respond to backfield flow.

MAN CHARGE TECHNIQUE

Again, we want a rolling start and a penetrating charge, except the alignment will shade the blocker. We teach the lateral alignment with the feet, and it is possible to have many different shadings. Initially, we teach a shading so the inside foot splits the stance of the blocker. We want to be eighteen inches off the ball to get room for the rolling start. The defender aims the charge for the numerals of the blocker. The idea is to knock the offensive man back, creating a new line of scrimmage behind the ball. It is vital to get a quick start and maintain a level charge with good leg drive. If that is accomplished, most of the battle is won.

We also want to teach the rushman to react on the move. Our defender makes contact with his shoulder and reacts to the key of the blocker. Should the blocker move inside, the defender brakes his charge and moves to the inside with the shoulders parallel (Diagram 8-7).

We also want an inside reaction for a pull outside, expecting the trap (Diagram 8-8). For the single block, the defender stops his charge and gets across the head of the defender (Diagram 8-9). He responds to the pass rush by accelerating to the passer.

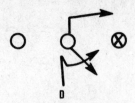

Diagram 8-7

Man Charge—Inside Reaction

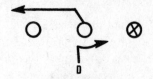

Diagram 8-8

Man Charge—Outside Pull Reaction

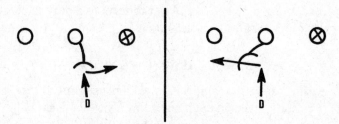

Diagram 8-9

Man Charge—Single Block Reaction

MAN CHARGE THROUGH RESISTANCE

We need to drill the defensive down lineman to meet resistance in the man charge. For this drill, we have a player hold a cylinder dummy and align the defender in his stance. The coach lifts the ball while barking a cadence and the defender takes off in a rolling start, aiming his charge for the middle of the dummy. A good level charge, quickness in the rolling start, force in the charge, and foot movement are checkpoints for an evaluation of the charge. As the drill progresses, we have the coach signal a direction that causes the defender to shed the block and redirect his path parallel to the line of scrimmage (Diagram 8-10). We utilize the man charge through

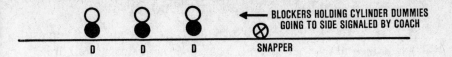

Diagram 8-10

Man Charge Through Resistance and Block Reaction

resistance every day (after teaching the man charge in pre-season) and in defensive practices during the season in weeks in which we plan to use it.

DRILLING MAN CHARGES LIVE

We align two or three blockers and have the coach signal them for the pattern and the starting count. Another player is assigned to lift the ball (Diagram 8-11). The defender makes his charge and attempts to react to the blocking pattern. We can add a back for a response to flow. This drill is utilized every day after it is introduced (on the third day in pre-season practice) and each week in-season when we plan to use man charges. In game weeks, blocking patterns can be tailored to the opponents. We do not take much time to teach block protection in conjunction with an aggressive charge. The defender will get to the blocker and learn through repetition how to get his hands on the blocker and work across his face. It will become automatic after a while; the defender learns to react to blocking keys and pressure.

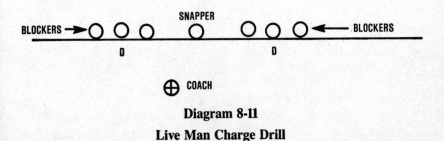

Diagram 8-11

Live Man Charge Drill

DRILLING AGAINST THE TRAP BLOCK

If you teach aggressive play for down linemen, you must accept the premise that you will be trapped sometimes. Well-drilled rushmen and other players in your defensive unit will minimize the damage that is done by traps.

We use this drill twice during pre-season and only in-season if we are having big problems with the traps, since group, team, and individual work against blocking patterns should provide us with enough work against traps. For this drill we align an offside guard or tackle and assign him to trap our defender, directing the frontside blocker into a trap pattern (Diagram 8-12). The defender must continue to make his aggressive charge, then react to the trap. He closes hard to the inside when he keys the trap (Diagram 8-13). He is to keep his shoulders square, move to the inside, and take on the blocker with a hard inside forearm into the sternum. It is necessary to work across the face of the blocker, and we advise the defender to work upfield to make this easier for him.

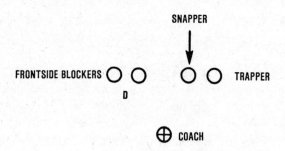

Diagram 8-12

Defending the Trap

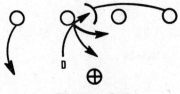

Diagram 8-13

Closing the Trap

DRILLING THE MOVE CHARGES

We use the slants, loops, quick arounds, stutters, and other move charges as surprise weapons. They have proven valuable as part of stunting maneuvers in conjunction with other defensive positions or simply as charge variations. The move charges, when employed in the proper situations and well executed, have won several games for us.

The teaching progression for move charges is the same as for gap and man charges. We make the move against resistance in the form of cylinder dummies, then work live. The move charge drills are carried out in the pre-season every other day after the moves are installed on the fourth day. In-season, they are drilled once each week for the weeks they are in the game plan.

TEACHING THE PASS RUSH

Down linemen must be your best pass rushers. You must use game-tested techniques to close and remove the pass blocker from the rush lane; otherwise your pass rush will not be consistently effective. The coach uses a dummy to represent the passer in the pocket. He walks the defender through his pass rush route, demon-strating the "moves" to be used. The first move is the hand swipe and around. The defender gets off the mark and strikes the blocker at the deltoid with his forearm or hand, then takes a swimmer's stroke with the opposite arm in order to slip past the blocker. It must be emphasized that the move is to be done on the run, with the rusher accelerating his feet throughout the charge. The other rush taught is the hit and jerk, where the defender runs straight for the middle of the blocker, making shoulder contact at the numerals, quickly pushing the elbow or shoulder of the blocker out of the rush lane, again accelerating the feet throughout the rush.

GAME-TESTED PASS RUSH DRILL

This is where you get individual coaching attention on the down lineman pass rush. For us the drill has yielded great dividends. Defenders are aligned against blockers so that they are pass blocked by the offensive linemen. The ball is lifted and the defenders attempt to get the rolling start, beat the pass block with one of the two drilled moves, and get to the marker designated as the passer. We ask the down linemen to use one or both of the drilled moves for their pass rush. We teach pass rush the fourth day of pre-season practice, drill it every day in the pre-season after that, and try to do it at least once every two weeks in the individual period during defensive practices in-season.

THE GAME LOOK 5 ON 2 DRILL

This is the individual period drill where we put all the charge and reaction fundamentals together. We drill this every day in the pre-season from the first day of practice on and nearly always once each week during the season. We set up a reserve unit of five linemen, including a center and another lineman behind him to take the snap. Two down linemen align properly and get off on the ball, reacting to various blocking patterns. In the pre-season a variety of play patterns are run by the dummy group. They get assignments from cards shown to them by the coaches. For game weeks, the patterns are those used by the opponents (Diagram 8-14).

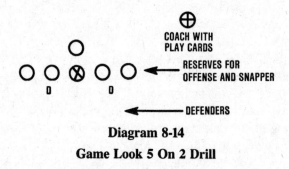

Diagram 8-14

Game Look 5 On 2 Drill

Down linemen perform agility drills in every defensive period in addition to defensive starts and charges through resistance. Tackling drills for the down linemen are the same as those used for defensive ends, except we only have them do the tackling form work on alternate practices, as they do not do as much open field tackling. We have the down linemen do 5 on 2 drills almost every practice and schedule the other drills on a rotating basis or as needed.

NINE

Game Tested Drills for Inside Linebackers

Although all defensive positions require discipline and good technique, inside linebackers and down linemen in our scheme tend to be more reckless than players at end, outside linebackers, or in secondary, who are more patient and deliberate in their style of play. Inside linebackers are frequently in position to make the tackle, since their alignment and pursuit patterns may make it difficult for the offense to block them. The defensive coach should be able to take advantage of the aggressive nature of these defenders; they must "get around the ball."

AGILITY DRILLS

After stretching exercises, the inside linebackers execute a series of agility drills. Agility drills for inside linebackers are carioca, shuffle wave drill, seat rolls, and shuffle over bags. (All these drills have been described in previous chapters.) No more than four at a time do three repetitions of each agility drill each time individual defensive drills are done, which is every morning in the pre-season and once each week during the season.

STANCE AND ALIGNMENT

Players align and get in stances improperly when they do not concentrate, and we found that our poor concentration in this phase of the game stemmed from a failure to impress the inside linebackers that they could not effectively carry out their responsibilities unless they aligned in proper positions and proper stances.

All inside linebackers are aligned across from a partner with a chalk stripe in between. The group representing the defense faces the coach and aligns with the hips fairly low, feet even, back straight, arms hanging loosely, weight on the balls of the feet. Since the linebackers are off the ball, they do not sink their hips nearly as low as the ends or outside linebackers.

The linebackers' feet are about two and a half yards back off the chalk stripe, which represents the line of scrimmage. They align with the nose on the inside eye of the partner, going from a stance shading the right side of the partner. When the coach is satisfied with the first group, he can hustle to the other side of the line and make the facing group the defenders. We only use this drill on the first day of practice. After the first day stance and alignment are reviewed early in each individual period as a part of other drills.

FORM TACKLING

Form tackling for inside linebackers is the same as for defensive ends, and the manner and frequency of the drills is exactly the same.

GAME-TESTED BLOCK PROTECTION DRILLS

The crucible of wins and losses has taught me that a young man can play linebacker if he can do two things: (1) get to the ball, and (2) shed blockers. That may sound like oversimplification, but all linebacker play stems from those two principles. You can assist a player who has an innate sense of getting to the ball by coaching and drilling him well in keys, movement, and technique, but there are many players who simply do not have that necessary "sixth sense" and, consequently, never become good linebackers. On the other hand, players with a fair amount of strength and explosive power can be taught to shed blocks.

On the first day of practice, each defender gets a partner to face him with a shield. The defender assumes his defensive stance across a chalk stripe. The coach selects one of the defenders and fits him into the shield with a forearm raise so that the defenders can see the proper method of shedding the block by using the forearm raise. (The player is instructed to step into the shield with a foot and to use the forearm on the corresponding side.) The forearm raise is simply the act of driving the forearm into the middle of the shield. The fingers must be relaxed when the defender starts the upward motion with the arm, since tensed muscles in the arm retard the speed of the blow. On contact, the thumb should be pointed to the ground. The opposite foot is brought up even with the lead foot while at the same time the opposite hand strikes the blocker's arm in an attempt to shed him. After several demonstrations, the coach gets across from the defenders and on command the players with shields thrust at the defenders and the defenders use the forearm raise. Each defender gets about five shots, then partners switch and the other group gets five turns. We use this drill each day of the first week of practice and then discontinue it.

A good variation of the drill is to do it live by having the blockers align in a stance and come out full blast at the defenders, who are executing the forearm raise. We use this drill beginning on the second day of pre-season practice, continue it every day during the pre-season, and use it when we need it during the season.

We also have the inside linebackers use the forearm drill on the seven-man sled. Each defender strikes each pad, shuffles to the adjacent pad and strikes it, and continues on for all seven pads. We use the opposite forearm and strike and shuffle back the opposite way. We use this drill on alternate days in the pre-season and infrequently during the season.

In order to drill for block protection against low blocks, we have the blockers come out and attempt to run through the ankles of the defenders. We ask the defender to get his hands on the defender and move his feet back if necessary. We emphasize staying square and remaining on the feet at all costs. If that is not possible, it is necessary to bounce up quickly. We use this drill in the third day of pre-season practice and on alternate days after that. In-season we rarely use the drill. In group situations and team defensive drills, we have the blockers cut our defenders if our film study shows us that the opponents have a tendency to do that.

We think it is necessary to prepare our inside linebackers to play so that their movement falls into three distinct conformations: (1) a key of the offense and a movement parallel to the line of scrimmage, crossing blockers, staying square and making the tackle where the ball crosses the line of scrimmage—this is commonly known as a *shuffle* pursuit pattern; (2) a key of the offense and a quick move to penetrate the line of scrimmage and then pursue the play—known as a keyed stunt move; (3) a move to penetrate the line of scrimmage on the snap of the ball—known as a stunt move.

SHUFFLE PATTERNS OF PURSUIT

The shuffle linebacker is generally aligned about three yards off the ball and may align in various shading positions on an offensive lineman or according to his own down linemen (stacked behind, splitting his own man's stance, etc.). We use the nose of the linebacker as an alignment reference. We may have him place his nose on the lineman's nose, either eye, or either ear. The shuffle linebacker can key an offensive lineman or a back. Some coaches go so far as to have the linebacker key a "triangle" of three players, but that is too complex at our level of play. An example of how a shuffle linebacker might key a lineman in front of him is illustrated in Diagram 9-1. He is to shuffle slightly behind the ball so as not to overrun it and to be prepared to come up to the line of scrimmage to make the tackle when the ball crosses the line.

The shuffle linebacker must be prepared to take on the blocker who comes after him by stepping up to close the hole and he must be prepared to shuffle behind the ball and cross the face of blockers attempting to cut him off. In meeting the straight ahead drive block, we want the defender to step into the blocker and force a collision by taking him on with an outside forearm raise, rolling the hips into the force of the blow. Immediately, the defender brings up the opposite hand and pushes the opponent away, reacting to the flow of the play. The defender can anticipate which way he will need to shed the blocker by determining which side the blocker is attempting to work his head to, then shedding the opposite way.

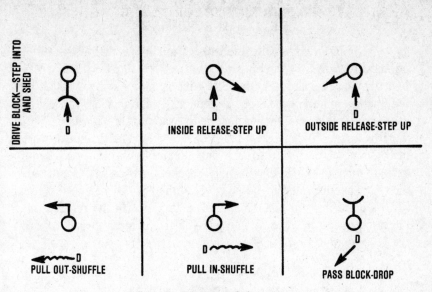

Diagram 9-1

Shuffle Linebacker Key Reactions

There is a larger school of thought among coaches who prefer that linebackers take blocks with the inside forearm, rather than use our preference, the outside forearm. I could fill many pages with a discussion on the merits and demerits of both methods, but our theory is that we want to force the offense to the sideline, so we play from the inside out. We adhere to that policy as a general rule; we break the rule only if absolutely necessary.

If the shuffle linebacker's key directs him to shuffle, he does so and remains behind the ball, taking on attacking blockers with an outside forearm raise into the sternum, then a quick push across the body with both hands. If necessary, the linebacker may give ground when working across a block, but he must remain shuffling with his shoulders square to the line of scrimmage, so he can react in either direction. If the ball is well outside the linebacker, he must turn his shoulders and run for a point of intersection somewhere beyond the line of scrimmage or until he is in such a position that he may square his shoulders and again shuffle.

GAME TESTED PROCEDURES FOR TEACHING SHUFFLE KEYING AND PURSUIT

We align two inside linebackers and have their keys align offensively. Our first teaching situation is to line up our linebackers in the basic setup and have them key linemen. Markers are set up so the linebackers can get proper alignment (Diagram 9-2). The coach carefully explains and then walks the linebackers through the pursuit patterns against the different reads of the keys. The linebackers are drilled on how they are to step and pursue as the key makes the various maneuvers. Each set of linebackers moves half speed and then full speed against each maneuver of the key (Diagram 9-3). The drill is done this way the first week of practice in the pre-season. During the season, if we are going to shuffle, we use the drill once in the individual period.

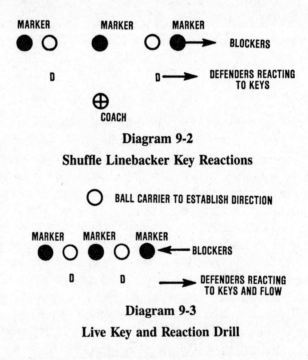

Diagram 9-2

Shuffle Linebacker Key Reactions

Diagram 9-3

Live Key and Reaction Drill

A progression of the drill places an offensive front and an offensive backfield composed of sophomore and reserve players, who run plays drawn up on play cards shown to them by a manager

(Diagram 9-4). This gets the linebackers reacting to the play and shedding the block. We do not tackle in this drill. Since we have a drill in connection with the down linemen that is similar to this drill, we only do this drill three times in the pre-season.

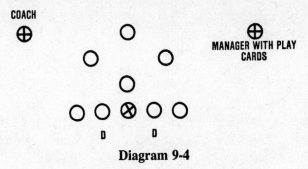

Diagram 9-4

Play Reaction Drill—Shuffle Linebackers

KEYED STUNT PURSUIT PATTERNS

Generally backs are keyed for the keyed stunt patterns, although it is possible to key offensive linemen. If the key directs to a certain side, the linebacker is directed to a penetrating movement, the most fundamental of which is the Scrape. The linebacker takes a lead step to the side and slightly up followed by another such step to bring the shoulders parallel to the line; if the key continues, the linebacker attempts to penetrate the line of scrimmage (Diagram 9-5) and make his play. If he is met by a blocker, he takes on the block with the outside forearm, and gets across the face of the blocker (Diagram 9-6), picking up the flow and shuffling behind the ball.

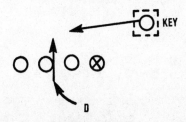

Diagram 9-5

Initial Steps for Scrape Movement

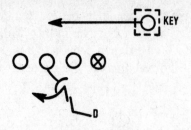

Diagram 9-6

Scrape Movement and Shed of Block

The second fundamental keyed stunt is the Plug, which is generally towards the center and is a good way to check the backside counter as well as get into backside pursuit. The Plug directs the linebacker to take two quick steps up and to the center; he does not continue on his penetration unless the ball is coming directly to him. The linebacker holds his ground for a moment and takes on any blocks with the inside forearm. He must not be turned but remain square and get into pursuit when he is certain the play has developed away from him; at this point he usually must turn and run so he can establish the proper pursuit angle which cuts off the ball carrier somewhere beyond the line of scrimmage (Diagram 9-7).

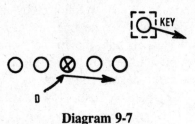

Diagram 9-7

Plug Move and Pursuit

GAME-TESTED PROCEDURES FOR TEACHING KEYED STUNTS BY LINEBACKERS

We align two inside linebackers and reserves who compose an offensive backfield. We key the backs and set up markers for our linebackers to use as guides for the keyed stunt maneuvers (Diagram 9-8). The coach signals the flow of the backs with a visual signal and

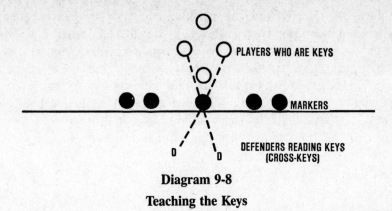

Diagram 9-8

Teaching the Keys

the linebackers react properly. We use this drill as a teaching drill the first three days after the Scrape and Plug are introduced and then discontinue it. We go back to it during the season once each week for weeks in which we plan to Scrape and Plug.

Next we have reserves fill out the front five of an offensive line in addition to the backfield. A manager holds play cards and the reserves runs live plays (no tackling) at our linebackers. The coach can check for proper keys, pursuit paths, and sheds. We do this drill three times in the pre-season.

GAME-TESTED WAYS TO TEACH STUNT MOVES

Unkeyed stunt moves penetrate the linebacker on the snap of the ball. The bane of a stunting linebacker is to overrun the ball (Diagram 9-9) and I have had this happen to my linebackers many

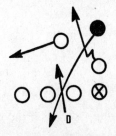

Diagram 9-9

Stunting Linebacker Overrunning Play

times. We decided that the penetrating linebacker had a better chance of recovering from a block or getting to a ball carrier if he hit the penetration route with the shoulders parallel to the line of scrimmage (Diagram 9-10). We insist that the linebacker take a stutter step parallel to the line and in the direction of the gap so he can hit the gap square. If he gets hung up in a block, he must brake his charge and get both hands on the blocker in order to get across his body and into an effective pursuit path (Diagram 9-11).

Diagram 9-10

Stutter Step and Stunt Move

DEFENDER HAS POSITION-
CONTINUES PENETRATION

DEFENDER HUNG UP-
CROSSES FACE OF BLOCKER

Diagram 9-11

Beating the Defender on Stunt Moves

GAME-TESTED STUNT MOVE DRILLS

The coach uses markers to set up the drill and takes a set of linebackers and walks them through stunt moves. When each move has been carefully explained, the set of linebackers will go through the move at the instant the ball is lifted. Each set of defenders gets about four shots. Once the players are confident of the move, we progress the drill so that the defenders must run through shield resistance to carry out the stunts (Diagram 9-12). The emphasis is on hitting the line of scrimmage hard with the feet moving. We step up the drill, using live blockers and having the defenders halt the charge and shed across the face of the blocker, if they are hung up. With experience, the defender will have the "feel" of when he has beaten the blocker; consequently, he will know when he can continue to accelerate into the backfield or when he must fight across the block.

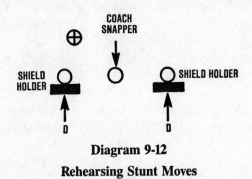

Diagram 9-12

Rehearsing Stunt Moves

We drill each stunt move in the pre-season on the day that the particular stunt is introduced and also review all previously learned stunt moves. We work against shield resistance each time we work the drill and use live work three times in the second week of pre-season work. During the season, we drill the stunts in the game plan, first just "shadow-boxing," reacting to the stunt itself, then against shields.

PASS DROPS FOR INSIDE LINEBACKERS

As a coach, you will not encounter the great passing attack every week. On the other side of that coin, as a result of today's emphasis, pass defense is a greater problem for the high school coach than ever before. When the high school passing attacks blossomed into pro sets and coverage reads, we began having a lot of trouble against the passing teams that were well drilled and possessed talented people at the skilled positions. In my case, the problem was not with the long pass; it was the short-and medium-range pass that chewed up ten to thirty yard gains that literally destroyed us. The deep coverage seemed adequate; it was the underneath coverage that needed shoring up. Our approach was to remain sound with our deep coverage and to improve underneath coverage by varying the coverage schemes and reemphasizing and better teaching pass defense by our linebackers. (Linebacker coverage is one of the weakest components of defensive play in scholastic football.)

There are countless coverage patterns in defensive football. Our approach is to teach underneath coverage as a zone principle; we can use elements of combination and man coverage to supplement, but we must understand and effectively utilize zone coverage.

We begin by dividing the field laterally so there are five points referenced on the spotted position of the ball and fourteen yards off the ball. These reference points are all given names (Diagram 9-13) and are spaced according to fractional distances from the spot of the ball to the sideline. A code system can be developed which has inside linebacker retreating for any of the five particular spots depending on the situation. But the most fundamental retreat for this inside linebacker is the path to the hook spot, fourteen yards deep and one-fourth of the way from where the ball is spotted to the

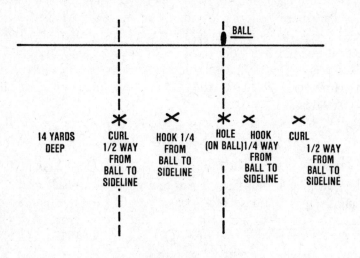

Diagram 9-13
Short Zones on Field

sideline. If the linebacker recognizes the pass, we want him to turn to his outside and retreat for the hook spot, keeping his eyes on the passer.

It is important to teach the concept that the hook spot is a reference, for the linebacker is retreating in that direction. Should the passer set to throw before the linebacker gets to his hook spot, the defender will turn and face him so he can react to the passer. Those who have underneath coverage responsibility should anticipate the passer by reading his eyes and reacting before the arm action tells them to; if they are wrong in their anticipation, at most a short pass is completed; more often they are correct and they have an excellent chance of getting to the short pass. With good progressive drill a good linebacker will become conscious of where the eligible receivers are in his zone, which will accentuate his mental "groove," helping him to better anticipate the delivery of the ball.

GAME-TESTED PASS DEFENSE DRILLS FOR LINEBACKERS

It is necessary that those who have coverage responsibilities be trained to react to the ball while it is in the air. Whether man for man, zone, or combination, a pass defense cannot be effective unless the defenders can get to the ball. Pass defense drills should teach the underneath defender to: (1) anticipate and judge the flight of the ball, (2) cover as great a distance as possible while the ball is in flight, (3) play the ball aggressively, (4) extend vertically for the ball as much as possible, and (5) teach the footwork and direction of the pass drop to the proper spot. There are literally hundreds of pass defense drills. We do not do a drill just for the sake of doing it and we do not have so many drills that we spend a great deal of time just organizing and learning them.

On the first day of practice, we set up a drill to teach the proper pass drop by using cone markers to mark the spot for our two backers and cones to mark the hook spots. Another player or the coach retreats as the quarterback and the linebackers retreat for the hook spots, turning and facing the "passer" if he sets to throw before the linebackers get to the hooks. We use this drill every day the first week of pre-season, three times in the second week, except we add a ball and have the defenders react to a soft lob pass (Diagram 9-14). We seldom use this drill during the season.

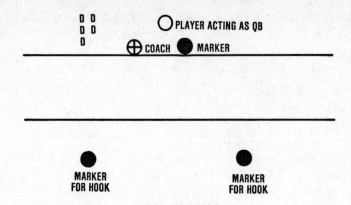

Diagram 9-14

Teaching Pass Drops (Changes According to Lateral Field Position)

For ball reaction, we initially set up the coach on a sideline midway between two chalk stripes that are ten yards apart. The linebackers are ten yards deep. The coach throws the ball to the middle or five yards to the outside of either linebacker. They are told to focus on the eyes of the coach and to break for the ball when his eyes indicate he will let it go. At first we like to make it relatively easy for the defenders to get to the ball. As the players improve, we can make it more difficult, eventually moving them back and widening them, then drilling the ball harder. Players waiting behind those active in the drill can shag any misses and give them to the player who missed, who can run the ball back to the coach while the next group lines up for its turn (Diagram 9-15).

The players align single file about twenty yards from the coach and run forward at half speed. The coach puts the ball in the air so each player can get several turns coming forward and breaking on the ball. The coach makes this drill more difficult as time goes on and varies it by having the players come forward and break on the ball. The drill gives the defender a picture similar to the one he sees on pass defense.

The coach uses the same setup for the deflection drill except that two players at a time run forward, one about five yards in front of the other one. The front player tips the ball to the back defender. They switch positions for each turn, giving each player three or four shots. We vary the drill by having the groups of two run laterally in

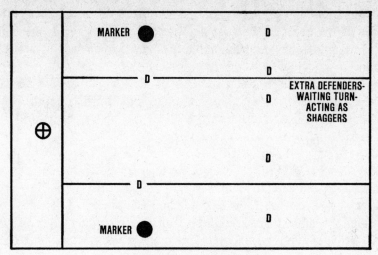

Diagram 9-15

Reaction From Lines

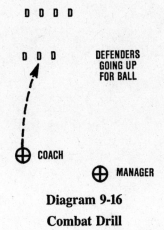

Diagram 9-16

Combat Drill

each direction. The front man tips it behind him. These "tip" drills are an excellent method of learning to adjust quickly to a deflected ball. Check your game films and find out how many tipped balls are intercepted.

The distraction drill is set up similar to the deflection drill, with a group of two approaching the coach. The coach releases the ball at the head of the first defender who ducks under the ball, requiring the defender behind him to concentrate on the flight of the ball.

The combat drill teaches the defender to compete for the ball with the receiver. A group of three, ten yards from the coach, plays the high lob pass (Diagram 9-16). This is also a good drill for teaching maximum vertical extension.

All pass defense drills can be expedited if each participant shags his ball and runs it back to a manager who is standing next to the coach, prepared to ready a ball for the next drill action. Plenty of footballs should be provided. When pass defense drills are well organized, a lot of action takes place in a short period of time. We do all the pass defense drills every day in the pre-season and once each week during the season.

TEN

Coaching Outside Linebackers with Game-Tested Drills

Four-deep defensive teams have taken what was once called a defensive end and replaced him with a linebacker by adding pass coverage and off-the-ball techniques to supplement his on-the-ball assignments. Three-deep teams have replaced a down lineman with an outside linebacker who can play off the ball and in the pass coverage, in addition to fulfilling the basic-on-the-ball responsibility.

We are fortunate in having a separate outside linebacker coach for our drills, but if you do not have enough coaches, it is possible to have your defensive end coach drill the linebackers for line of scrimmage work and your inside linebacker coach drill them for off the line work and pass defense. The position of outside linebacker requires more discipline than any other position in defensive football.

AGILITY DRILLS

After stretching exercises, the outside linebackers execute a series of agility drills. Agility drills for outside linebackers are carioca, shuffle wave drill, seat rolls, and shuffle over bags. All these drills have been described in previous chapters. No more than four at a time do three repetitions of each agility drill each time individual defensive drills are done, which is every morning in the pre-season and once each week during the season.

FORM TACKLING

Outside linebackers use the same form tackling drills as the other players.

LINE OF SCRIMMAGE TECHNIQUE FOR OUTSIDE LINEBACKERS

We align the defender so his feet are one yard off the hands of the offensive blocker (initially the tight end, although it it possible to play the outside linebacker on slots, wings, or other linemen), with the nose of the defender on the inside eye of the blocker. It is possible to vary the depth of alignment or the shadings on the blocker. The defender has his feet even, weight on the balls of his feet and his hips are in a low position, much lower than is the case for the linebacker who plays off the ball. The defender is looking directly at and is keying the blocker. He is prepared to deliver a two-hand uppercut with open hands into the sternum of the blocker.

At the same time, we want him to mirror the step of the blocker, stepping with the corresponding foot. If the offensive player is attempting to block our man, he neutralizes him with the step and uppercut and pushes him out of the way and picks up the flow of the backs. If the blocker is blocking down, the defender moves to the inside and keeps his shoulders square, alerting for another block from inside out; he should make it very difficult for the blocker to release to the inside. If the blocker releases outside, the defender shuffles out and remains in a low position, looking for another block or secondary reaction. The defender must fight the double team by neutralizing the man in front of him and then stepping directly into the drive blocker with the near foot and simultaneously striking him in the sternum area with a forearm raise.

All secondary reactions are based on the flow of the backs. The outside linebacker remains on the line of scrimmage with his

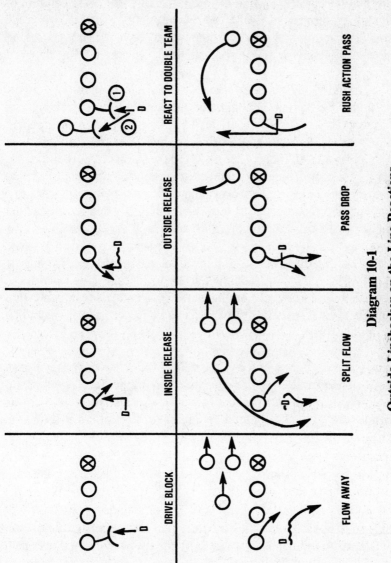

Diagram 10-1

Outside Linebacker on the Line Reactions

shoulders square. He is to take on blockers coming from the inside by stepping and striking with the inside forearm into the sternum area, keeping the shoulders parallel to the line. He must shuffle inside to close the play that is going to his inside, being careful not to sink (to turn to the inside and pursue) until he is certain that the ball is past him. He defends the wide play by shuffling to the outside, remaining slightly behind the ball, thus forcing the play wider.

Initially, the outside linebacker is taught to play the quarterback on the option, although this assignment can be altered for different situations. We coach the defender to remain in position and allow the quarterback to get slightly past him, then to shuffle outside remaining slightly behind, ready to make the tackle if the quarterback keeps, or to turn and run if the quarterback pitches. If the flow is away, the outside linebacker delays slightly, then turns and runs for a point that is twenty yards deeper than the spotted position of the ball (we call this the tunnel), all the time observing the flow. This defender actually becomes a final safety man on runs to the opposite side or an intermediate cushion on action passes to the other side. If the flow is split, we caution the outside linebacker to be responsible for the widest receiver coming out of the backfield, dogging him until the ball is in the air, at which time he plays the ball, or until he is certain it is a run, at which time he pursues the ball.

If the outside linebacker recognizes a drop back pass, he makes his pass drop. If it is an action pass to his side (generally we define this as one in which the passer is outside his tackle's lineup position), we initially instruct to rush the passer recklessly on his inside shoulder. The line of scrimmage reactions are shown in Diagram 10-1.

STANCE AND ALIGNMENT DRILL—LINE OF SCRIMMAGE LINEBACKERS

The linebackers pair off and face each other across a chalk stripe. The coach faces the defense and checks defensive alignment. We have them align so the nose is on the inside eye of the opponent with the feet one yard from the hands of the opponent's three- or four-point stance. We want the feet even, about shoulder width apart, the back straight, and the arms hanging loosely inside the knees. The hips are low and the eyes are focused on the opponent, since the man facing the defender is the first man who can block him. The linebacker takes a right shade, then a left shade. Then the coach runs to the opposite side and the other group works the stance and alignment. We do this drill on the first day of pre-season practice and repeat it on the second day of practice, then eliminate the drill, as we can check alignment and stance in other drills.

GAME-TESTED DRILLS FOR BLOCK PROTECTION

We align shield holders across from defenders with a chalk stripe between them. The defender assumes the stance and an inside eye shade. On the command of the coach, the shield holder thrusts the shield at the defender. The defender is taught to mirror the first step of the blocker. If the blocker steps with his outside foot, the defender delivers a two-handed open-hand uppercut to the middle of the shield, then brings the opposite foot up and throws the blocker aside. The blocker keeps the shield waist high, takes three turns with the right foot as the first step and three turns with the left foot as the first step, then switches roles with the defender. We introduce this drill the first day of pre-season practice and do it every day for the first week.

We expand on the block protection drill by having the blocker go live against the defender. The blocker comes off the line and uses a different starting foot for each turn while the defender delivers his two-hand uppercut for each thrust, mirroring the starting foot of the blocker. Each man takes six shots.

READING THE BLOCKERS ON THE LINE OF SCRIMMAGE

We use the live drill so that the coach can signal the blocker to come off either foot and drive block the defender or attempt an inside or outside release (Diagram 10-2). On the inside release, our defender should shuffle one step to the inside and get his hands on the blocker, keeping the shoulders square and the hips down. We do not want a "clean" inside release, particularly if the defender has an inside eye position (Diagram 10-3).

The outside release is played by a shuffle out for one step, getting the hands on the blocker, keeping the shoulders square and

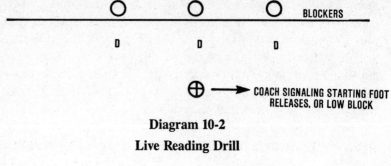

Diagram 10-2

Live Reading Drill

Diagram 10-3

Avoiding Clean Inside Release

the hips down. The defender must look back to the inside after either release. We also have the blocker come off and target his charge below the knees of the defender. The linebacker must get his hands down on the blocker and keep his feet free. If necessary, he can shoot the feet back and give ground a bit. He must not get turned or tangled up in the block. The on-the-ball reading drill is done every day in pre-season and during the season when the outside linebackers align on the ball as part of the game plan.

GAME-TESTED DEFENSIVE MACHINE DRILLS

Outside linebackers need drills that combine and isolate block protection and movement. The individual chosen to play this position must have enough strength and technique to neutralize and shed the block, and must be mobile enough to get himself in position to make the play.

We use the seven-man sled to drill block protection and movement for outside linebackers. Seven outside linebackers align on the sled pads. Each player assumes a stance so that his feet are a few inches from the bottom of the sled. Since it would be necessary for the eyes to focus away from the target if we started on a sight signal, we have the coach who is located on the other side of the sled give a voice command that causes each player to strike the pad with a two-hand uppercut, coming off with the right foot at the same time the uppercut is delivered, then coming up parallel with the other foot. We take ten shots with the right foot first, then ten shots with the left foot first.

We also have each player strike each sled pad with his right forearm as he extends his right foot, then shuffle to the adjacent pad and strike it, carrying out the routine on all seven pads. After all the players have worked down the sled with the right forearm, they return in the opposite direction using the left forearm on each pad. We do the machine drills for outside linebackers almost every time we have individual defensive drills.

OFF-THE-LINE TECHNIQUES FOR OUTSIDE LINEBACKERS

Outside linebackers also play off the line of scrimmage and are located at an outside position or directly in front of an offensive blocker. If there is no blocker to key, the flow provides the complete reaction picture, and the outside linebacker makes the same reactions to flow as for the basic line of scrimmage technique. These responses are indicated in Diagram 10-4. The difference in assignment is frequently that the outside linebacker who is located to the outside and off the ball is responsible for outside containment rather than the end and may have the pitch man on the option. Also, the farther removed the defender is from the line of scrimmage, the farther behind the ball he shuffles, so as to keep the interception point of tackler and runner in proper perspective—minimizing overrunning the ball.

For outside linebackers who are aligned off the ball but directly in front of an offensive blocker, we instruct the defender to key the blocker and pick up the flow for a secondary reaction. In this case, the initial key is the same as that for the inside linebackers who are keying linemen (Diagram 10-5). The secondary reactions to flow are the same as those taught for the line of scrimmage techniques. Stances are similar for the off the line linebackers, except it is not necessary or desirable to have the hips as low, providing better vision.

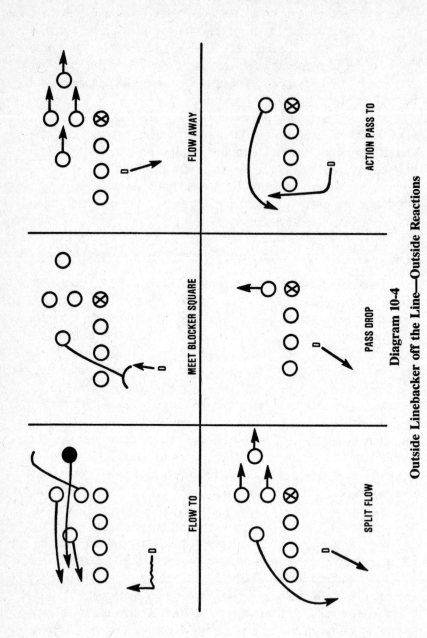

Diagram 10-4

Outside Linebacker off the Line—Outside Reactions

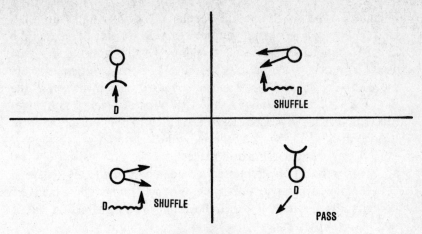

Diagram 10-5

Response to Keys—Off the Line—On a Lineman

STANCE AND ALIGNMENT—OFF THE BALL TECHNIQUE

Stance and alignment are taught for off-the-ball variations by using the same setup as was used in the line of scrimmage technique. Each time a new alignment variation is introduced, we use the stance and alignment setup to teach the location for the outside linebacker and then discontinue the drill after the first day.

GAME TESTED DRILLS FOR FOREARM RAISE BLOCK PROTECTION

If the outside linebacker is aligned off the ball or if the blocker runs a distance greater than two yards in order to make contact, we teach the forearm raise as block protection. The drills employed are the same ones used to teach the inside linebackers this form of block protection.

GAME-TESTED PROCEDURES FOR TEACHING OUTSIDE LINEBACKERS TO KEY AND PURSUE IF ALIGNED OFF THE BALL

We align two outside linebackers and have their keys align offensively. Markers are set up so the linebackers can get proper

alignment. The coach carefully explains and then walks the linebackers through the pursuit patterns against the different reads of the
keys. The linebackers are drilled on how they are to step and pursue
as the key makes the various maneuvers. Each set of linebackers
moves half speed and then full speed against each maneuver of the
key. The drill is done this way the first week of practice in the pre-
season. During the season, if we are going to play off the line, we
use the drill once a week in the individual period.

A progression of the drill places part of an offensive front and
an offensive backfield composed of sophomore and reserve players,
who run plays drawn up on play cards shown to them by a manager
(Diagram 10-6). We do this drill three times in the pre-season and do
not tackle in the drill.

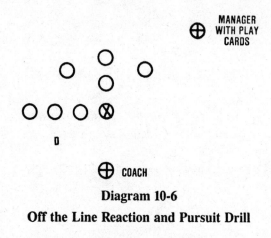

Diagram 10-6

Off the Line Reaction and Pursuit Drill

In playing off the ball and to the outside of the offense, it is
helpful to have two lines of linebackers facing the coach, reacting to
the various moves of the coach who establishes: (1) flow to either
side; (2) a play breaking through the middle; (3) a drop back pass;
(4) an action pass to either side (Diagram 10-7). We progress this
drill by taking a full backfield with play cards and establishing flow
(Diagram 10-8), being particularly careful to pay a lot of attention to
situations in which the blocker crosses the line of scrimmage and
attacks the linebacker. This constitutes a unique problem for the
defender, since there is so much room to the outside and there is not
as much congestion on the line of scrimmage. A special coaching
effort is made to teach the defender to come up and aggressively

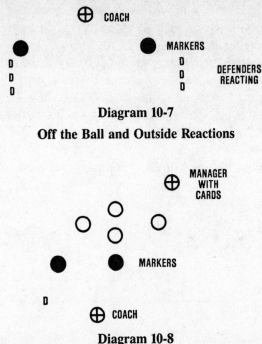

Diagram 10-7

Off the Ball and Outside Reactions

Diagram 10-8

Off the Line and Outside Reaction and Pursuit

close the angle, meeting the blocker with the shoulders square, simultaneously stepping at and delivering the inside forearm into the sternum area. We must do individual off-the-line outside work at least three times in the pre-season and once each week during the season if we anticipate using a lot of that particular alignment variation.

STUNT MOVES FOR OUTSIDE LINEBACKERS

Outside linebackers can stunt from any alignment. The concept of the stunt maneuvers by an outside linebacker is classified as: (1) a movement on the snap of the ball that commits the defender to cross the line of scrimmage and attack the offense in the backfield, (2) a very slight one- or two-step movement to relocate the defender quickly to a point where he is able to fulfill the functions of a linebacker, but with a different responsibility (such as outside containment, changed option responsibility, variation in pass drops, etc.), and (3) the same initial key response, but a different responsibility to flow, such as different option responsibility, or change in containment assignment.

Examples of penetrating movements by outside linebackers are illustrated in Diagram 10-9. We want to take a slight direction step prior to penetration, which helps us to stay square while carrying out the stunt. The objective is to get penetration and force the offense in the backfield. If the penetrator is met by a blocker, he drives through the block unless he is hung up, in which case, he stops his charge and gets across the face of the blocker (Diagram 10-10).

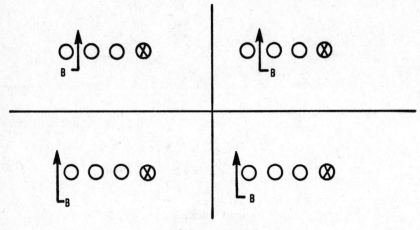

Diagram 10-9

Penetrating Outside Linebacker Stunts

Diagram 10-10

Clearing Blocker if Caught in Block for Penetrating Stunt

Examples of the quick relocation and assignment change stunt maneuver are illustrated in Diagram 10-11. The defender is still playing parallel to the line of scrimmage and shuffling.

An example of the stunt maneuver in which there is merely a secondary assignment change is illustrated in Diagram 10-12. In this

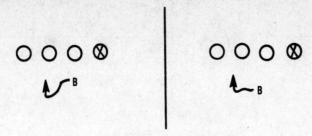

Diagram 10-11

Relocation and Assignment Change Maneuver

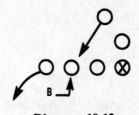

Diagram 10-12

Assignment Change

particular case, the outside linebacker may be assigned the dive back rather than the quarterback on the option.

GAME-TESTED DRILLS FOR OUTSIDE LINEBACKER STUNTS

If you do not work with intensity on the penetrating stunt moves, they will not be beneficial in game situations. We found that just calling the stunt and telling the defenders where to go did not cut the mustard; the defenders were carrying out the maneuvers very softly, which was disastrous.

In teaching the stunts, we align the backer facing the coach, using markers as reference points. The player is instructed as to the move and is walked through each move as it is introduced. The moves are next executed full speed on a command from the coach (Diagram 10-13). We use the stunt move drill on the day the stunt is introduced in the pre-season, and quickly review previously introduced stunt moves. We use the drill full speed against air and against shield blockers the first week and go through stunt moves live three

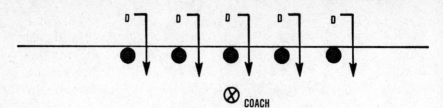

Diagram 10-13

Stunt Drill—Through the Gap

times the second week of pre-season practice. In game weeks we review the stunt moves to be used for the given week against air and against shields at full speed, but not live.

PASS DROPS FOR OUTSIDE LINEBACKERS

Coverage is just as important for outside linebackers as it is for inside linebackers. In general, the outside linebackers need more range to get to their pass drops than the inside linebackers. Again, our approach to pass defense is to remain sound with our deep coverage, supplementing with good underneath coverage by varying coverage patterns and emphasizing good pass defense by the linebackers.

We divide the field laterally so that fractional demarcations are noted (Diagram 10-14) at depths of eight and fourteen yards. It is possible that outside linebackers may cover any of the spots that are noted, but the most fundamental retreat is to the flat, eight yards deep and three-fourths of the way from the spotted position of the ball to the sideline. If the linebacker recognizes the pass, we want him to turn to his outside and retreat for the flat, keeping his eyes on

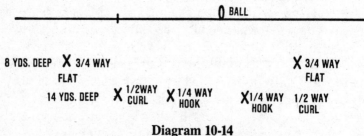

Diagram 10-14

Pass Drop Reference Chart

the passer. It is important to teach the concept that the flat is a reference, for the linebacker is retreating in that direction. Should the passer set to throw before the linebacker gets to his flat, the defender will turn and face him so he can react to the passer. We believe that those who have underneath coverage responsibility should anticipate the passer by reading his eyes and reacting before the arm action tells them to. If they are wrong in their anticipation, at most a short pass is completed. More often they are correct and they have an excellent chance of getting to the short pass. With good progressive drill a good linebacker becomes conscious of where the eligible receivers are in his zone, which accentuates his mental "groove," helping him to better anticipate the delivery of the ball.

TEACHING PASS DROPS FOR OUTSIDE LINEBACKERS

We position two outside linebackers by using markers and a line of scrimmage and have them turn to the outside and walk to their flat areas. After each player has walked to his area, we take two at a time and have them drop quickly to the flat when the coach raises the ball. The players retreat until the coach cocks the ball as if to throw it. When that happens, the defenders turn and face the coach, get their hips down, and become ready to react to the eyes of the passer. Each player goes through the drill quickly and then switches lines (Diagram 10-15). After four repetitions from each side, the coach moves the ball to one side, walking the linebackers through the appropriate reactions for moveout passes, having each player go through two reactions from each side for moveout passes both toward and away from him (Diagram 10-16 and 10-17). This drill is used in the first three days of the pre-season and is then discontinued. We use a faster paced pass drop drill if we feel our pass drops

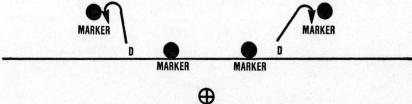

Diagram 10-15
Pass Drop Drill—Outside Linebackers

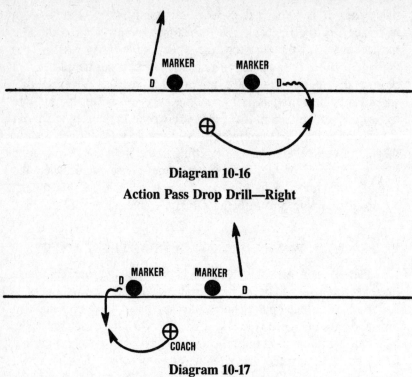

Diagram 10-16

Action Pass Drop Drill—Right

Diagram 10-17

Action Pass Drop Drill—Left

are weak. A reserve player is assigned to quarterback the drill. He drops back and quickly sets. He releases the ball so the defender can play his eyes and break on the ball. When we vary the drops of the outside linebackers in terms of position, alignments, or coverage responsibilities, we go through the teaching drill again in the individual period, employing the variations in assignments.

PASS DEFENSE DRILLS FOR LINEBACKERS

Drills used for ball reaction for the outside linebackers are the same as those used for inside linebackers, discussed in the previous chapter.

GAME-TESTED OPTION DRILLS FOR OUTSIDE LINEBACKERS

The drill is set up by placing markers and using a quarterback and trail back. The outside linebacker is initially taught to play static and let the quarterback go beyond him slightly. He learns to guage the quarterback's path and get a feeling as to when to start his shuffle and stay inside the quarterback. The greater the distance the quarterback is off the line of scrimmage, the greater the distance the linebacker remains inside of him. If the quarterback pitches, the linebacker turns his shoulders and runs in pursuit (Diagram 10-18).

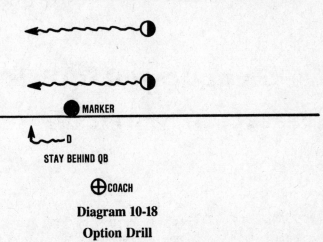

Diagram 10-18

Option Drill

We use the option drill three times the first week of practice and three times the second week of practice. The drill is used in season when we are preparing for an option team and it is altered so that the particular kind of option and any alignment or assignment variations are employed (Diagram 10-19).

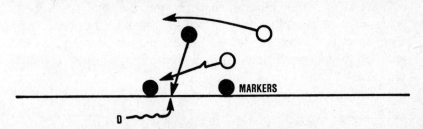

Diagram 10-19

Option Variation—Dive Responsibility

ELEVEN

Game-Tested Individual Secondary Drills

You do not need to coach very long to learn that your secondary can lose games faster than any other part of your squad. A lot of coaches and nearly all casual followers of the game recognize that a poor secondary will give up lots of "bombs" and yardage to the pass offense; but if you carefully analyze the big runs against you, it is obvious that an ineffective secondary can hurt you just as badly in that phase of the game. We refer to our secondary as the Shell because it constitutes our reserve force and must contain the offense. The personnel in the secondary must be carefully selected and even more carefully drilled. Mistakes there will often result in a score or very poor field position for the defense; the best forcing unit will be broken several times in each game; only with an excellent secondary will the offense be stopped.

STANCE AND INITIAL MOVEMENT DRILL

It is easy to ignore the importance of stance in your secondary people. They are located a long way from the ball and the stances must be higher so they can see. I have been beaten by both the run

162

and the pass because my secondary was not alert and in position to make the play, but also because my secondary was too quick to make a commitment to an initial movement of the offense.

In order to prevent too quick a reaction in the wrong direction for the secondary, we think a "delay" step is necessary. Although I have known coaches who have taught this initial step as a step up, the vast majority teach it as a step back and to the outside. In order to make this step properly, it is necessary to have a good stance. A second benefit of a good stance for a secondary defender is that it tends to keep him mentally alert.

For this teaching drill, all secondary defenders align on a chalk line, facing the coach. There is a slight flex in the knees, but otherwise the stance is tall. Eyes are focused on the coach. The left foot is behind the right foot in an approximate heel and toe arrangement, and the feet are no wider than shoulder width. When the coach raises his hand, all players step to the outside and back with the left foot, then bring the right foot back. After four turns using this movement, the players position the right foot back and step out and back with the right foot on the visual signal by the coach. This is the maneuver we want secondary people to use on the snap; it helps them read the key before going to a reaction. We use this drill every day in the first week of pre-season practice and then discontinue it because we check stance and initial movement in other drills.

GAME-TESTED DRILLS FOR SECONDARY BLOCK PROTECTION

Coaches probably pay less attention to teaching and drilling secondary defenders in block protection than any other position; yet if one of these defenders is knocked on his back, it is usually more costly than it is for any other position. We align each defender facing a partner across a chalk line. We begin by having the players walk through the maneuver. The blocker approaches the secondary defender and the defender comes to meet him, thrusting his hands into the chest of the blocker while he is simultaneously taking a lead step. The extension of the hand rip is the roll of the hips into the blow and the follow up with the back foot so the feet will be parallel. Each player walks through the block protection three times and then we go live. The initial distance apart is ten yards. We only walk through the drill the first two days of pre-season practice and from then on we go live and do the drill every time we have individual defensive drills. The fourth day of pre-season practice and every time we do the drill on succeeding days we give each player an additional three shots against a blocker attempting to block him low. It is important to get the hands down on the blocker and the defender may give ground slightly, but it is imperative not to get turned or knocked down.

TACKLING DRILLS—GAME-LIKE SECONDARY SITUATIONS

Tackling drills for the secondary are the same ones used for other positions with two additions. We station a ball carrier behind a blocker and have them both run through two dummies spaced five yards apart. Both offense and defense start at the same time with a twenty-yard distance between them. The defender advances cautiously and plays the blocker with the hand rip, then plays the ball carrier. In playing the blocker, it is important not to get turned and to remain square so the ball carrier is indecisive as to his cut; once the blocker is neutralized the defender positions himself so that he is on either numeral of the ball carrier, effecting a slight shade position. This puts the tackler in excellent position to make the tackle if the cut is straight ahead or to the shaded side; if the cut is away from the shade, the defender should be able to flatten out the course of the ball carrier and force him to the sideline. Coach secondary men to always remember that the sideline never misses a tackle.

The open field sideline drill consists of markers and a ball carrier, blocker and defender (Diagram 11-1), offense and defense initially about twenty yards apart. On command the offense advances between the markers and the sideline, with the defender positioning to cut them off at the pass. It is imperative that the defender force the play into the sideline and position himself so that there will not be an easy cutback. We initially teach the secondary to play this conservatively, using the hand rip and going through the blocker when the blocker commits himself, then driving through the inside numeral of the ball carrier. We use this drill and the conservative approach for two days the second week of pre-season practice. On the third day of the second week, we introduce the defenders to the aggressive approach, by instructing them to gauge

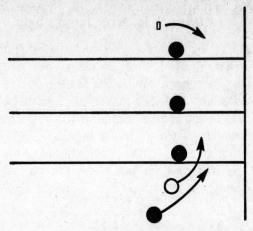

Diagram 11-1

Open Field Sideline Drill

the situation until the time is right and then to attack the blocker by running through his inside knee and extending the body on the ground.

When properly executed, this maneuver will pile up the blocker and the ball carrier. With good drill work, the defender can usually expect to at least slow up the ball carrier so that the pursuit forces him out of bounds (Diagram 11-2). We continue this aggressive drill for two more days in the pre-season, then any time the open field sideline drill is used we allow each player to elect which approach to use for any given situation.

Diagram 11-2

Attacking Blocker and Ball Carrier Aggressively

GAME-TESTED METHOD FOR BODY CONTROL IN DEEP COVERAGE—RUN THE LINES

We introduce this drill on the opening day of practice and do it every time we have defense. The players line up in groups of three on chalk lines ten yards apart. The coach has them assume a stance and then raises his right hand. The players step out and back and then turn the shoulders and retreat on the lines. The coach then signals the opposite direction, which causes the players to plant, roll the shoulders to the opposite sideline, and retreat along the same lines (Diagram 11-3). The eyes are focused on the coach throughout the maneuver. Each group gets three shots in this drill.

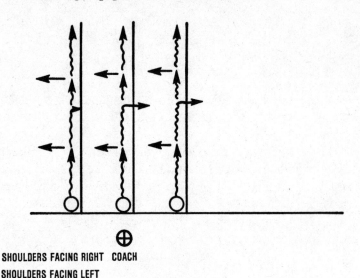

SHOULDERS FACING RIGHT   COACH
SHOULDERS FACING LEFT

Diagram 11-3

Run the Lines

DROP ANGLE DRILL

We use this drill every time we have defensive practice. In our zone concept, we teach the secondary to take an angular movement while going from the aligned position on the snap of the ball to a deep retreat line on the field. We want the defender to gain depth while gaining width in order to cover the field. The players are aligned in groups of three on adjacent ten-yard chalk stripes, facing the coach. On command, the coach points to a certain direction, which triggers the defenders to drop to the adjacent ten-yard stripe (Diagram 11-4). When the defender hits the adjacent stripe, he plants and takes a drop angle in the opposite direction, keeping his eyes on the quarterback throughout the drill. He zigzags from mark to mark until he has gone the width of the field. The drop angle we want is three yards width for every yard in depth. All zone coverages are worked out geometrically on that basis. The coach can use the drill to help him evaluate secondary candidates. It tells him a lot about footwork, an essential for a good pass defender.

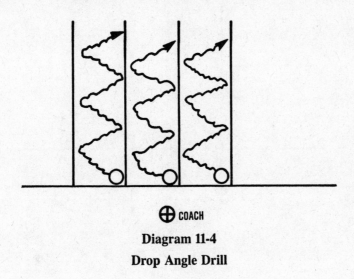

⊕ COACH

Diagram 11-4

Drop Angle Drill

GAME-TESTED BEAT DRILL

It is inevitable that a secondary defender will be occasionally beaten deep. There is a way to teach him to recover and still break up the sure touchdown pass. This is a good drill for the situation in which a defender "feels" a receiver running through his zone and recognizes that he cannot keep a deep cushion by using his drop angle to get to the deep line. If such is the case, the defender breaks off his route and literally chases the receiver in a man for man set up. He stays with the receiver and reads his eyes.

His teammates alert him verbally when the ball is in the air by yelling "ball," and he can find out when to react by reading the eyes of the receiver and turning to the ball and thrusting his hands in the air at the last possible instant (Diagram 11-5). It is surprising how quickly the defender can improve in the beat drill. We add some spice to it by purposely underthrowing the receiver and having him come back on the ball, forcing the defender to do the same.

Another coaching point in the drill is to instruct and drill the defender in cutting off the receiver for situations in which the

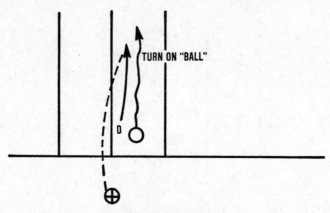

Diagram 11-5
Beat Drill

Diagram 11-6
Cutting Off Receiver's Angle

receiver is taking an angle and has greater acceleration in that direction. The defender is taught to intersect the path of the receiver and the ball while looking for the ball (Diagram 11-6). The defender will get the feel of the situation by repetition in the drill set-up. We run the beat drill every other day in the pre-season practice and about once every two weeks during the season.

GAME-TESTED BALL DRILLS FOR SECONDARY DEFENDERS

We use all the ball drills that the receivers and the linebackers use, except that we use every drill every day. There are two additional drills that we incorporate for the secondary in the ball drills.

We have defenders line up on chalk lines twenty yards apart and position a player in the middle but at the intersection of the boundary and a chalk stripe. The defenders are seven yards deep. Either the coach or a reserve quarterback can be the passer. The receiver takes off and the defenders retreat on the chalk stripes, with the shoulders turned to the receiver. A depth cushion is maintained by the defender so that he is not beaten deep. The passer releases the ball so that it will come down at a depth of thirty yards. The defenders should learn to react to the ball when the passer drops his front arm while the passing arm is rolling up (Diagram 11-7). As the

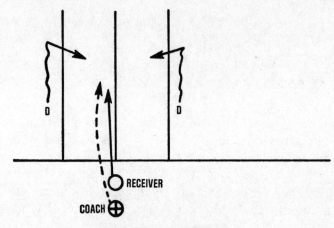

Diagram 11-7
Ball Reaction From Lines Drill

defenders improve, we release the ball sooner and on a tighter arc so the defenders learn to react more quickly. We use this drill every time we practice defense.

We also have players retreat on chalk stripes twenty yards apart in groups of three and throw the ball deep behind them. They must learn to turn and sprint for the ball. We encourage the defender to take his eyes off the ball when he judges it is over his head, turn and sprint to the ball and then relocate it with his eyes, just as a good centerfielder would do. We use this drill three times in the pre-season and only when we think it is necessary during the season.

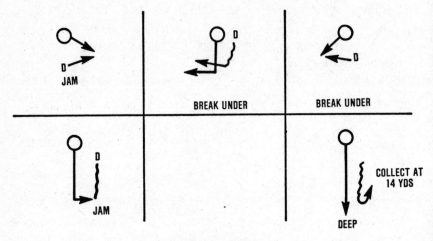

Diagram 11-8

"Freeze" on Wide Receiver

GAME-TESTED MAN AND COMBINATION COVERAGE DRILLS

There are times when we use elements of man-to-man coverage in conjunction with a zone. As a result, it is necessary to design a drill that will incorporate our man principles. We give examples here by showing "Freeze" and "DIO" coverage patterns (Diagram 11-8 and 11-9). We have the receivers go through the various patterns we wish to cover by putting the routes on cards and running the defender through his paces against all possible cuts. We use this drill when each specific coverage variation is taught in the pre-season and

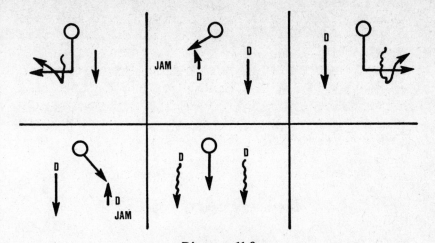

Diagram 11-9

"DIO" (Double Inside-Outside) Coverage

review it a couple of times. We use the drill in-season in weeks when the game plan calls for a particular variation. There are literally hundreds of man and combination schemes that can be used in this drill.

DEFEATING THE CRACK BACK AND STALK BLOCKS

Secondary defenders will have the crack back and stalk blocks to contend with. Unless they are drilled well, plan to have lots of long gains against your deep defenders because they will not tackle well when they are on the ground.

We set up a back and a blocker with a shield, with markers to give us starting positions. The shield man comes down on our defender as the back goes wide. The defender must learn to "feel" the block coming, depress his hips, and meet the blocker by stepping with the near foot and using the hand rip into the sternum area, crossing the face and keeping the shoulders square (Diagram 11-10). We set this up the second week of practice and repeat it once, reviewing in-season if we think it necessary.

For the stalk, we use the same set up, except we are in position where our assignment is to key the blocker and cover deep on action to our side. The shield man will break down and attempt to pass

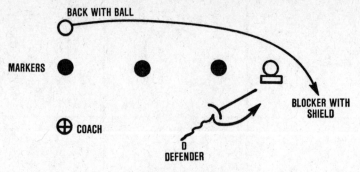

Diagram 11-10

Defending Crack Back Block

block the defender. When the defender recognizes the run, he must break down and step into the defender with the hand rip. The idea is to neutralize the defender and shed him, remaining square, coming up under control to make the play (Diagram 11-11). Shedding is the act of pushing the defender aside after he has been neutralized by the shock of the hand rip.

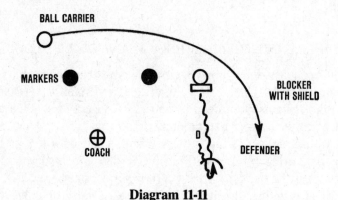

Diagram 11-11

Defending the Stalk Block

THREE-DEEP ROLLING ZONE—KEYS, ALIGNMENTS, REACTIONS

I am going to focus on the essentials of three-deep zone coverage as it applies to action passes and drop back passes. We will describe how the zone is to be rolled on action. You must understand that four-deep schemes and many variations of the three-deep coverage are possible; this is a base and if the players understand and can execute this base, it is not difficult to teach them necessary differences in other coverage patterns.

We align defensive halfbacks (we call them Anchors) seven yards deep and eight yards outside the position of the ball. If the offense has a receiver positioned wider than that, the defender adjusts his width one yard inside the receiver except he does not align closer to a sideline than eight and a half yards (halfway from the hash mark to the sideline). The safety (we call him the Swing) is ten yards deep and splits the two outside eligible receivers except he does not align outside a hash mark. Defensive backs align with the outside foot slightly back (the middle defender opens up to the wide field).

Outside secondary defenders key the widest receiver on their side for the first two steps, then pick up the flow of the backfield. They must learn to be conscious of receivers depth all across the field. The middle secondary defender keys and picks up the flow of the backs. He must learn to feel the depth of the receivers all across the field. In time your good defenders will know the lateral and vertical location of all receivers.

Next is the geometry of the football field—an overlooked part of the pass defense. Because of where the ball may be located laterally, the reaction distance of the backs will vary. If a ball is thrown from a hash mark deep to the far sideline, the back on that side has a greater time to react to the ball than the back on the other side would if the ball were thrown deep to his sideline. Consequently, we have deep defenders drop at angles to deep retreat lines before they take vertical drops. The retreat lines depend on where the ball is located laterally.

On a drop back pass, the outside defenders take drop angles to "streak" lines and the middle deep defender takes a drop angle to a "pipe" line. Geometrically, these lines are placed so the proper distance between them allows the defenders to have enough room to react and play the ball properly. The streak lines are halfway from the position of the ball (after the snap) to the sideline, but no closer to the sideline than eight and a half yards (halfway from the hash to the sideline), and the pipe line is located on the ball except no wider than four yards inside either hash mark. Diagrams 11-12 and 11-13 indicate where the retreats are located on the field.

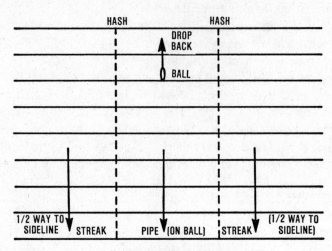

Diagram 11-12

Deep Retreat Lines—Ball in Middle

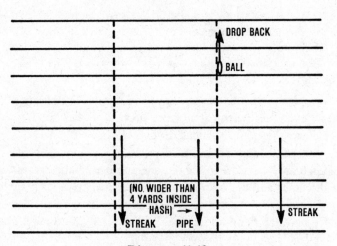

Diagram 11-13

Deep Retreat Lines—Ball On Hash

The drop angles to the retreat lines are three yards of lateral movement for each yard of depth. It is preferred by most coaches that the defenders retreat by backpedaling when they hit the retreat lines, keeping a depth cushion all across the field, playing the passer so that when he drops his front elbow, they will react to the ball. It is also possible for the defenders to turn towards the passer and retreat on the proper lines, playing the passer.

For the action pass, the outside defender will probably see a release by his key; if the ball and the flow are toward him, he will level off and cover the flat. With the ball coming to him, he must get a width cushion of one yard all the way to the sideline (he must be wider than the widest receiver in the flat. Should his key block on the line of scrimmage, the defender will alert for the run, coming up under control, keeping his shoulders square in order to force the ball into the sideline. He should meet blocks with the hand rip. If he keys a wide receiver, the offensive player will probably release for the run and the pass. The defender must read the flow and come up to play the run a bit more cautiously in that situation. His advantage is that he is aligned wider and has more time to come up. If the flow is away, the defender on the outside will take a proper drop angle for the backside streak line. If it is a pass, he will retreat on the streak line, except he will not take a drop opposite the way the passer has

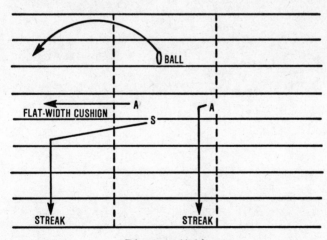

Diagram 11-14

Action Pass Coverage

moved (moving his streak line straight behind him in many cases). If it is a run away from him, the outside deep defender will take a pursuit angle to the ball.

The middle deep defender will key and react to flow. On a run, he will come up cautiously and force the runner to redirect to a sideline so the pursuit can catch him. The middle deep defender must not be blocked off his feet. If it is an action pass, the defender will take a drop angle to the frontside streak and retreat on that line, keeping a depth cushion all across the field. In order to get to the streaks, the middle deep defender may have to deepen for wide receiver sets. Diagram 11-14 shows coverage.

The execution of drill work to teach deep coverages will be covered in the following chapter.

TWELVE

Preparing Defensive Groups with Game-Tested Methods

Defensive group work provides the transition from individual fundamental drills to full team work. It is an important phase in each practice because we are creating an environment in which there are teammates to work with and more offensive positions to react to. In essence we are adding distractions that tend to distort the techniques the player has learned in the previous individual drill period. This is where the player learns to gain the "feel" of the subtle relationships necessary to disciplined defensive play, the cornerstone of sound defense.

5 ON 4 DRILL

This is certainly a game situation drill—one of our best. It is for inside linebackers and down linemen. We have two groups composed of five linemen and a full backfield manned by reserves who will run the plays. A manager is assigned to show play cards to each group (Diagram 12-1). The center for each group is responsible

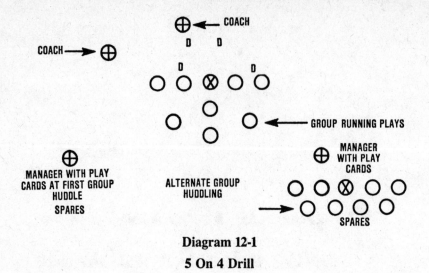

Diagram 12-1

5 On 4 Drill

for retrieving the ball after every play and carrying it to the line of scrimmage for all plays. All dummy team players are listed by teams on a note card before practice. When it is time for the drill, the coach yells the names of the two dummy squads and the players align quickly with their managers and run through the plays. The coaches for the down linemen and inside linebackers can be right on the spot coaching and making corrections.

The drill is full speed contact without tackling. Plays are directed inside the offensive tackles. The first day of pre-season practice we use twenty minutes for this drill, and every defensive session after that we run it for eight minutes. We use the drill once a week during the competitive season. We run the first unit about two thirds of the time and the second unit gets about one-third of the drill work. When the second unit runs the drill, we use the first stringers on one of the scout squads.

All the personnel assignments and changes must be listed before the coaches take the field. You can see the reason for good organization as we do not allow a lot of time. During twice-a-day sessions, we use plays that we expect that season's opponents to use, varying the formations, and blocking assignments daily so we can introduce variations in keys, movements, assignments, alignments, and stunts (Diagram 12-2). In the regular season, we run plays in the

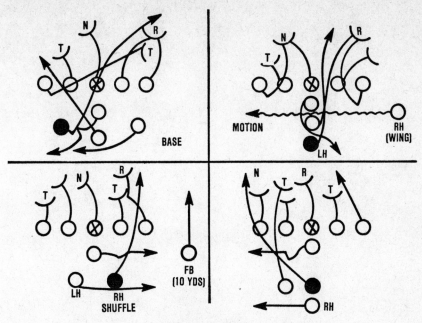

Diagram 12-2

Sample 5 on 4 Play Cards

way that we expect our opponents to run them. We do not regularly film or videotape this drill, but we have recorded it from time to time. If the drill is recorded, place the camera behind the defense.

THE GAME-TESTED 11 ON 4 DRILL

Outside linebackers and defensive ends are participating in this drill at the same time we are running 5 on 4 with the inside linebackers and down linemen. We prefer to do the drill in two sections if enough personnel are available (Diagram 12-3).

A scout squad is assigned for each section and this must be done before practice. The coaches yell out the names of the scout squad and they align quickly and prepare to run the plays. If ends and outside linebackers flop according to wide side of the field or formation strength, they can alternate sections for the drill work. The first unit gets two-thirds of the work and the second unit will work the remaining third of the period. First and second unit players work

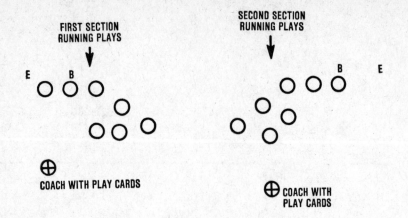

Diagram 12-3

11 On 4 Drill—Two Sections

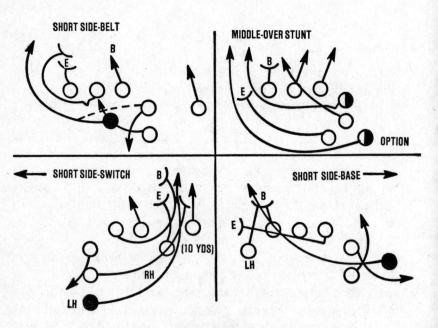

Diagram 12-4

Sample Play Cards 11 On 4

offense when the other unit is working defense. We take twenty minutes the first day of practice and eight minutes in every defensive session after that, which amounts to every day in the pre-season and once a week during the season.

On the play cards the coaches list position of the ball as to hash, defensive technique, alignment, or stunt desired. We use basic formations and base techniques for the first practices (Diagram 12-4), and incorporate new techniques as they are taught. In-season the play cards are drawn so that the formation, blocking assignments, and frequency tendencies are reflected. We want to make our "looks" as close as possible to what our opponents will provide. Each coach can run his own play cards and each dummy team is made up of four backs, a guard, tackle, and end. We emphasize off tackle and outside plays in the drill, occasionally using the action or dropback pass. Our outside people get enough work in pursuit for inside and opposite side plays in the 11 on 8 drill and in team defense. The drill is full speed contact without tackling.

TEACHING SECONDARY COVERAGES

This is a teaching period in which the secondary coach walks the Shell through coverages for pass actions (Diagram 12-5). It is used on a lined-off field. The coach goes through the drop and action passes in both directions from the left hash, middle of the field, and

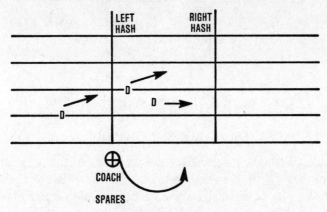

Diagram 12-5
Secondary Coverage Walk Throughs

the right hash, directing the personnel to react, take correct drop angles, and get on proper retreat lines for assignments. First, second, and sometimes third units can go through coverages in every period. We do this drill at the same time the outside and inside front groups are drilling.

We teach the new coverages and review previous ones each day in the pre-season. In game weeks we go over the coverages necessary for the game plan. Occasionally we station receivers in position so the defenders can align properly on the snap of the ball (Diagram 12-6). The first day of pre-season practice we spend a great deal of time walking through the base coverage alignments and assignments; after that we only get eight minutes per session of our coverage walk throughs. This is an excellent teaching period and should prepare the secondary for full scale pass defense.

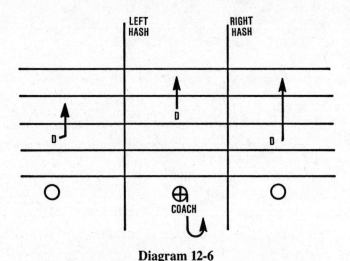

Diagram 12-6

Coverage Walk Throughs With Receivers Added

GAME LOOK 11 ON 8 DRILL

This is the best defensive drill we have. At the same time we are doing this drill, the secondary and an alternate set of linebackers are taking part in the skeleton pass defense drill. We assign two full scout squads on note cards before practice. We also list these squads on the blackboard before practice, which facilitates the organization.

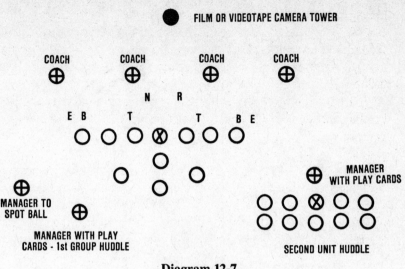

Diagram 12-7

Drill 11 On 8 Drill

A manager is assigned to spot the ball and another is assigned to showing play cards to each scout squad (Diagram 12-7).

We sort the plays according to hash marks so we can work plays from right, middle, and left hashes. On the play card is listed the defense to use (Diagram 12-8). All the coaches are positioned behind their defenders and can make corrections on the move. The drill is full speed without tackling. In the pre-season, the plays are a hybrid of ones we might expect to see during the coming season. Each day's plays are set up so that the various formation alignment adjustments, stunts, reads, and technique variations are used at the appropriate time. During the season, we take the plays from the scouting report.

We make a tremendous effort to use the formations, plays, and blocking assignments with the frequency which we expect our opponents to run them. The drill is twenty minutes in length and we give the first unit ten minutes work, then trade the linebackers with the pass defense so our second unit can work the second ten minutes. It is sometimes possible to give the third unit work for a few minutes at the end of the first period and the beginning of the second period. We can use first unit ends and down linemen for offense while the

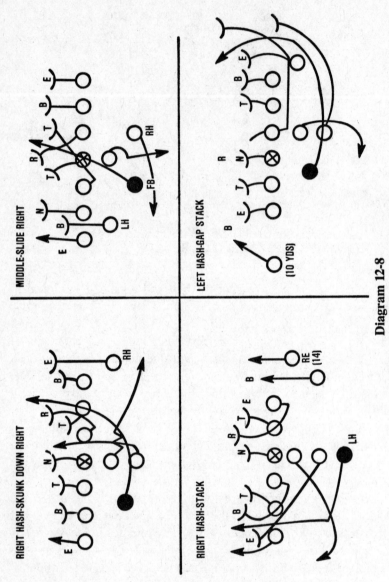

Diagram 12-8

Sample Play Cards 11 on 8 Drill

second unit is working defense and vice-versa unless we are working a unit pass rush drill for tackles and ends at the same time. We videotape or film the drill from behind the defense. The drill is done every day in the pre-season and twice each week during the season. In a ten-minute period it is possible to run twenty to twenty-five plays.

GAME-TESTED SKELETON PASS DEFENSE DRILL

I don't think you can have good pass defense unless you run some version of this drill. Individual defense drills will not develop the field and personnel relationships you must have with pass defense and scrimmage will not give you nearly enough pass defense work. While the first unit linebackers are working on the 11 on 8 drill, the second unit linebackers work pass defense with the second unit Shell. Reserves and the first unit Shell are listed on a note card according to position and assigned to run the pass patterns. Each unit consists of end and four backs. If personnel permits, we assign three dummy units; one runs pass plays from the right hash, one from the middle of the field, and a third runs pass plays from the left hash. Cards are drawn for each unit with the plays drawn that the defense is most likely to see from the various lateral positions. If we have only enough personnel for two dummy units, one runs two plays from the right hash, then one from the middle; the other runs

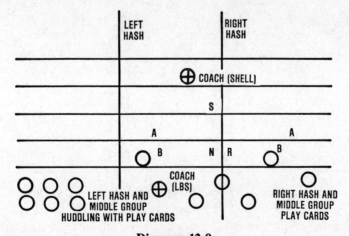

Diagram 12-9

Skeleton Pass Defense Drill

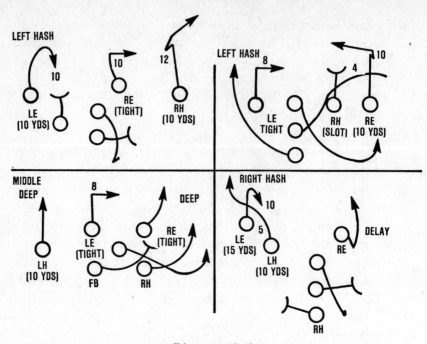

Diagram 12-10

Sample Play Cards—Skeleton Pass Defense

two plays from the left hash, then one from the middle (Diagram 12-9).

We run a sampling of the plays we expect our opponents to use against us in the coming season. During the season, we use the scouting report to determine how to draw up the patterns from the various formations and hashes (Diagram 12-10). We take great care in researching our opponents and getting a good "picture" for our pass defense. The coach calls coverage changes and variations in the drill. After ten minutes, the first unit linebackers trade places with the second unit linebackers and we use the first unit Shell, using the other Shell people and reserves to man the dummy squads. Two managers shag balls and return them to quarterbacks so the drill works smoothly.

I would not recommend recording the drill unless it is possible to use 16 MM film and locate the camera at an elevation of forty feet; otherwise the action is too spread out for effective evaluation. We run this drill seven times in the pre-season and twice each week during the season.

GAME-TESTED UNIT PASS RUSH DRILL

Although we do quite a bit of individual pass rush work, there is no substitute for working the rushmen together as a unit. We use this drill four times in the pre-season period, but we do not have enough personnel to use it during the season. When the first unit down linemen and ends are working the 11 on 8 drill, the second unit works the pass rush drill. They change drills after ten minutes. We use five reserve linemen, a fullback, and a quarterback for the dummy squad (Diagram 12-11).

Diagram 12-11

Unit Pass Rush Drill

Play cards are drawn up so that drop back and moveout passes are run. For the third and fourth sessions we also put in draws and screens. A manager shows the cards, and coaches are assigned to perfect the pass rush techniques introduced and drilled in the individual defensive periods (Diagram 12-12).

PERIMETER DRILL

We use this drill twice during the pre-season and discontinue it after that. It is designed to get the secondary and the ends working as a team. We instruct the players to employ full speed contact and tackling. The drill is scheduled in conjunction with the 11 on 8 drill by combining second team ends and Shell while the first unit ends are working on the 11 on 8 drill. The units alternate after ten minutes. Reserves and players not actively engaged in the defensive phase of

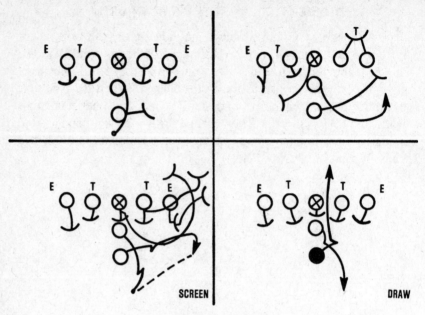

Diagram 12-12

Unit Pass Rush—Sample Cards

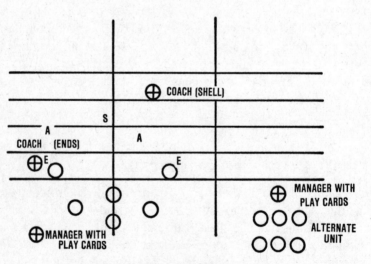

Diagram 12-13

Perimeter Drill

the drill will form two or three units to run wide plays from both hashes and the middle of the field (Diagram 12-13). Play cards are drawn up for each unit so that the frequency of direction of the various lateral field positions will be what we want it to be (Diagram 12-14). Occasionally we sneak in a running play or an action pass in order to keep our defenders honest.

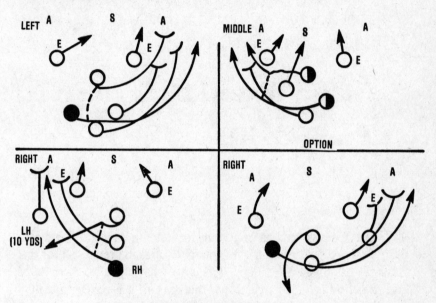

Diagram 12-14

Sample Play Cards—Perimeter Drill

After many years of research, experimentation, and revision, we arrived at our present, effective organization approach for defensive group drills.

THIRTEEN

Game-Tested Defensive Team Drills

Full teamwork is as important for defense as it is for offense. While offense is largely a question of timing, the relationships that must be established for good defensive team effort are developed over a period of many weeks. For that reason, it is easier to build a good offense than a good defense. The first step in having a good defense is aggressive individual play, but team defense is proper position, implying confidence in teammates, which enables each team member to execute his assignments with skill and enthusiasm.

READY LIST

At one time, I used the scouting report to draw up play cards of the opposition, then took the cards on the practice field and shuffled through them when we did defensive teamwork against a scout squad. The other coaches had no way of knowing which play was coming up, we could not coordinate our blocking assignments for the scout squad to use against a particular variation of defense, we did not have the proper frequency, field, down and distance, or special situation set up for our defense. The ready list took care of all these problems.

Our "ready list" is a script that determines every situation and play in a defensive scrimmage. We set up the situation so that the offense has down and distance, hash mark, yard line, and formation tendencies on each play. In the first week of pre-season practice we make play cards and note hash mark situations, but we do not prepare a ready list. In the second week of pre-season practice, our defensive teamwork consists of what a typical opponent will do in the given down and distance and field positions. There are twenty-six plays on all of our ready lists.

In preparing the ready list during the season, we work with film breakdowns and scouting reports in order to help us to prepare the defensive game plan, alert sheet, and ready list. We use a down and distance summary that is compiled on the basis of at least three scouting reports (Diagram 13-1). We have found that we can get a good idea of what the opponent prefers on the tough third or fourth down short and long yardage situations. We go through the scouting worksheets carefully (Diagram 13-2) in order to cross-reference down and distance tendencies with specific field tendencies. Some opponents may not stay with long or short yardage probabilities as the field position changes.

All scouting reports are filed with a hash mark summary sheet that helps us to determine what the opponent will do in the different lateral field positions (Diagram 13-3)—a definite aid in defining a game plan.

We use at least two opponent films and all scouting reports of opponent games for which we do not have films to build a formation breakdown chart (Diagram 13-4). Each game that is analyzed is noted in a different color on the charts. We also note all opponent blocking assignments, backfield action, and pass patterns, being particularly careful to determine how the opponent attacks defenses similar to ours. It is also helpful to break down the film of the previous year's game between ourselves and the coming opponent. If we play an opponent early in the season, we use films of later games in the previous season. When we are breaking down film early in the week, we can also get an idea of the opponents' strengths in personnel, although the really thorough study of personnel cannot take place until later in the week.

Down and distance summaries supplemented by over-the-field tendencies, hash mark breakdowns, formation summaries, knowl-

First Down (8–10)			Second Down (4–7)			Third Down (0–3)		
Long	*Medium*	*Short*	*Long*	*Medium*	*Short*	*Long*	*Medium*	*Short*
WR 28 To	WR 22 +4		TWR DBP	WL 16)0	WR 31 W +2	IG-OL	WL-49T	WL 31W
+6			Inc	+8		DBP-C +12	+1	+2
WL 44P +9			WL DBP Co +22	WR 25P +3	WR 31W +1	IG-OL Scr RT. +4		WR 33 +1
WR 29Pa			WL DBP Co +22	WR 25P +3	WR SOR Inc	WR-WB		WR 31W +3
Inc			WR 29 Pa Inc	WR 40TT +5	WR-SOR Inc.	Ctr −4		WR 44 +3
WR 170 (33F) + +12			Wr DBP Inc	WL 44P +4				WR 25 +1
WR 25P −1			WL 49To +6	WL 44P +5 TD				
WL 44P +5								
WL 44P (Fum)								
WR 170 (33F)+2								
WR 33 +1								
WR 25CB								
Pass Co +38								
WR WB Ctr −2								
WR 34 +5								
WL 16)0 (32F) +7								
WR 22+6								
WL 40TT +2								
WL 44P +6								
WR 34 +2								

Fourth Down

Long	*Medium*	*Short*
	WR 25CB	WR 31 W
	(Fly)	+1 TD

Diagram 13-1: Sample Down/Distance Summary
Mortonsville Vs. Wayne 9/20/xx

edge of opponents' plays, blocking patterns, pass routes, and a general idea of personnel strengths and weaknesses help us to formulate a defensive game plan (Diagram 13-5), which states the

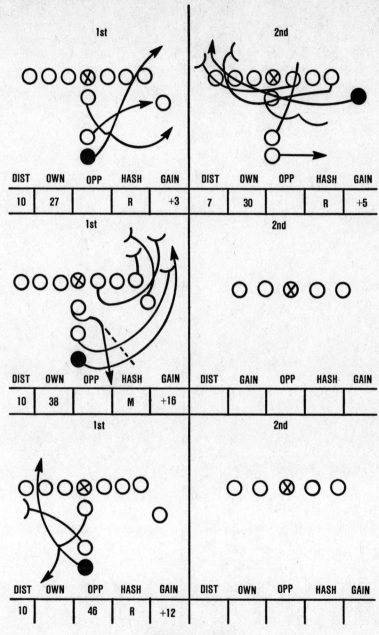

1st

2nd

DIST	OWN	OPP	HASH	GAIN
10	27		R	+3

DIST	OWN	OPP	HASH	GAIN
7	30		R	+5

1st

2nd

DIST	OWN	OPP	HASH	GAIN
10	38		M	+16

DIST	GAIN	OPP	HASH	GAIN

1st

2nd

DIST	OWN	OPP	HASH	GAIN
10		46	R	+12

DIST	OWN	OPP	HASH	GAIN

Diagram 13-2

Scouting Worksheet

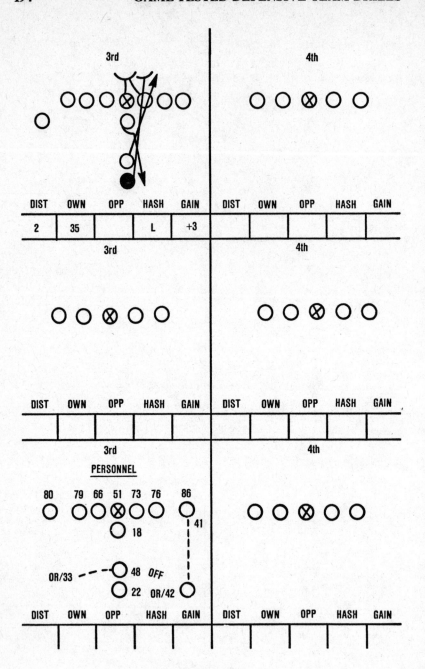

	3rd						4th			
DIST	OWN	OPP	HASH	GAIN		DIST	OWN	OPP	HASH	GAIN
2	35		L	+3						

3rd

4th

DIST	OWN	OPP	HASH	GAIN		DIST	OWN	OPP	HASH	GAIN

3rd

4th

PERSONNEL

DIST	OWN	OPP	HASH	GAIN		DIST	OWN	OPP	HASH	GAIN

Diagram 13-2 (cont.)

Left	*Middle*	*Right*
WL 160 +8	WR w8 Toss +6	WL 44P +4
WR 28 Toss +6	WL 44P +9	WL 44P +5
WR 25P +3	Tw R DBP Inc	WR 25P −1
WR 29 Pass Int.	WR 170 (33F) +12	WL 44P +8
WR 170 (33F) +12	WL 44P (Fum)	WR 25P +3
WR 33+1	WR 31 W +1	WR 22 +6
WR 33 T +4	WR Spr Out Right Inc	WL 40 TT +4
WL DBP Inc.	WR 34 +5	WL 49 Toss +4
IG-OL Scr. Rt. Comp +4	-WR WB Ctr −4	WR WB Ctr −2
WL 44P (Fum)		
WR 33T +4		WR 31 W +3
		WR 25 CB (Fly) 0
		WR 31 W + 1 TD
		IG-OL DBP Domp −12
		WR SO Right Inc
		WR 22 +4

Diagram 13-3: Hashmark Analysis Mortonsville vs. Wayne 9/20/xx

W—Wayne
H—Hutchinson
L—Largo

		33 (2)—L		
		33 (3)—W		
WBC (2)—L		33 T (1)—L	25 CB (3)—L	
WBC (2)—H	22 (4)—W	33 T (3)—H	25 CB (1)—W	39 (2)—L
WBC (2)—W		33 T (1)—W		29 (3)—H
	34 (4)—L	31 W (4)—L	25 P (3)—L	170 (lead) (5)—H
28 To (4)—L	34 (5)—H	31 W (5)—H	25 P (6)—H	170 (33 F) (3)—L
28 To (1)—W	34 (2)—W	31 W (3)—W	25 P (3)—W	170 (33 F) (4)—W

		DBP (3)—L		
SO Left (1)—L		DBP (3)—H		29 Pass (2)—L
SO Left (1)—H		DBP (4)—W	SO Rt. (1)—H	29 Pass (1)—H
SO Left (3)—W	Pass (3)—H	25 CB Pass (2)—L	SO Right (1)—W	29 Pass (3)—W
	34 (1)—L			49 To (2)—L
	34 (2)—H	40 TT (3)—W		49 To (3)—H
16 O (32 F) (3)—L	34 (4)—W	31 W (1)—L		49 To (3)—W
16 O (32 F)—H	44 P (3)—L	31 W (1)—W	43 (5)—L	35 (2)—L
16 O (32 F) (2)—W	44 P (3)—H	32 (3)—H	43 (3)—H	35 (2)—H
16 O (Lead)—W	44 P (5)—W	32 (3)—W	43 (3)—W	35 (3)—W
DB Pass (2)—L				
DB Pass (2)—H				
DB Pass (3)—W				

Diagram 13-4: Mortonsville Offensive Formation Analysis

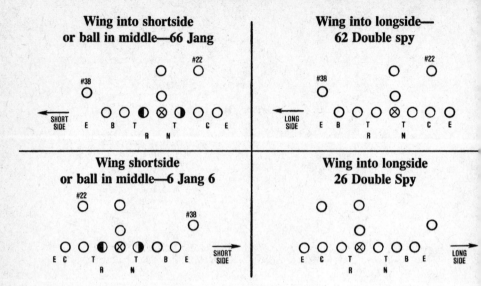

Within 4 yards of Hash is considered hash

62 Double Spy or 26 Double Spy on Wing into long side

Stunts: Occasional Bird Dog if formation long side or Over in same
   situation (called once in four from the bench)

Bull goes with #38 Wing (No Shift) Cat away

Short Yardage:
   3rd and 3 or less (up to our 40)
   4th and 3 or less (inside our 40)
   Stack Pop—Stack Pop Down into short side away from Wing

3rd and Long (4th and Long inside our 40):
   87 or 78 Double Walkaway
   ⅓ of the time Double Mad Dog
   or Bird Dog into formation on wide side
   Shell—Solid

Pro Sets: (on other than long yardage)— "Bandit" Mike plays fill
   and drill; Rover plays rake.

Twins: 87 or 78 Cover on inside receiver—Shell "Roger" or
   "Louie"

Diagram 13-5: Mortonsville Defensive Game Plan

defense we want to use for each specific situation. We make an alert sheet that directs each position to make the technique modifications necessary for all defensive calls. There is also emphasis on how to respond to what the opponent does best (Diagram 13-6).

Ends: Wide end wide side; left in middle—Squeeze all wings, tight end into short side—play pitch man on all options—alert for screens to left on pro set on long yardage; end away from wing must alert for long WB reverse—guard will trap; squeeze tackle on "Twins"; Crash on "Over"

Tackles: 66—Press on Wing side, Jang away; 26—Press, G-C gap on 2 side. Stack Pop—Pinch; alert for Mad Dog—Stutter and Bird Dog—Slant—*Trap only to Wing*; draw only on 3rd and long from pro set

Inside Linebackers: Cross key FB and HB—Scrape and Plug. *Spy* on 26 or 62—CLUC is Buz on action passes; can change PADs to shuffle/shuffle if hurt by tackle trap. Will trap into wing; screen on pro set long yardage to our left; draw only 3rd and long from pro set. Stack Pop on short yardage; they favor FB Wedge (down if short side is away from wing); Bird Dog or Over—formation long side; Mad Dog or Bird Dog into pro set on 3rd and long. Pro sets—normal yardage—Bandit—fill and drill by Mike and Rake by Rover.

Outside Linebacker: Bull on TE onside of Wing #38 (sub is #26). Play Ogle; Cat Eagle—Ogle on Tackle on 2 side. Alert for double walkaway call—Bull wipes off on over call; Wing and end will double Bull on power. Cat cover on inside slot on Twins.

Shell: Steady—Roger or Louie on twins; Solid on double walkaway—alert for out and up after setup.

General alerts: Trap into wing
Drop Back Pass, screens and draws and 25 Power from pro set
HB Pass
Only sprint from wing to our left

Diagram 13-6: Mortonsville Defensive Alert Sheet

Ready List—Mortonsville

Seq.	Down	Dist.	Own	Opp.	Hash	Formation	Play	Defense	Result	Index
			Yd. Line							
A	1	10	20		M	WR	25 P	Skunk	+4	#1
B	2	6	24		R	WL	44 P	Skunk Down	+5	#2
C	1	1	29		M	WR	31 W	Stack Pop	+1	#3
D	1	10	30		M	WR	WBC	Skunk	−3	#4
E	2	13	27		L	WR	29 Pass	Skunk Down	Inc.	#5
F	3	13	27		L	IG-OL	DBP	Slide Dbl Walk	Comp +16	#6
G	1	10	43		R	WL	49	Skunk Down	+3	#7
H	2	7	46		R	WR	33 T	Skunk	+1	#8
I	3	6	47		R	WL	40 TT	Skunk BD Rt.	+6	#9
J	1	10		47	R	WL	160 (32)	Sk. Down-Over	+8	#10
K	2	2		39	L	WR	17 LO	Skunk Down	+4	#11
L	1	10		35	M	WR	34	Skunk	+1	#12
M	2	9		34	L	WL	16 LO	Skunk	0	#13
N	3	9		34	L	WR	SO Left	Skunk	Comp +8	#14
O	4	1		26	L	WR	31 W	Stack Pop Down	+1	#15
P	1	10		25	L	WR	29 Pass	Skunk Down	Inc.	#16
Q	2	10		25	L	IG-OL	29	Skunk Down	−2	#17
R	3	12		27	R	IS1-R Twin	Scr Rt	Slide DBL Walk	Inc.	#18
S	4	12		27	R	WL	DBP	Slide Cover	Inc.	#19
T	1	10	20		M	WR	32	Mad Dog	+7	#20
U	2	3	27		L	WR	28 Tos	Skunk D-BD Left	+5	#21
V	1	10	32		L	WR	17 LO	Skunk Down	+3	#22
W	2	7	35		R	WR	170 (33)	Skunk	+2	#23
X	3	5	37		R	WR	SOL	Skunk	Comp +8	#24
Y	1	10	45		M	WL	16 LO	Skunk	+1	#25
Z	2	9	46		L	WL	40 TT	Skunk	+3	#26

Diagram 13-7—Offensive Ready List

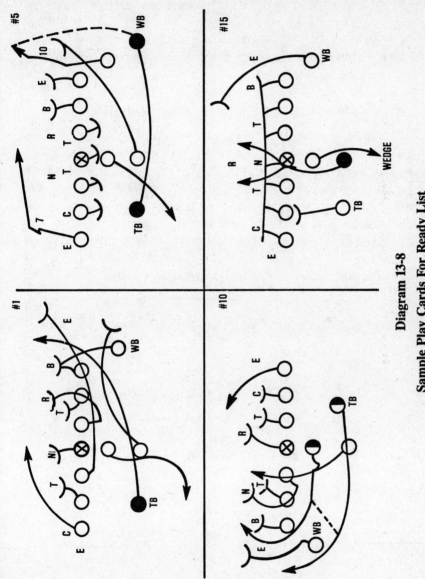

Diagram 13-8

Sample Play Cards For Ready List

When we have established the defensive game plan and alert sheet, we are ready to build our script for defensive scrimmage. We take great care in making the ready list since we want to structure our scrimmage to be as close to the game as we can make it. When the ready list is completed (Diagram 13-7), we draw a play card for each listing we have made (Diagram 13-8), which completes our preparatory work for the ready list.

GAME-TESTED DEFENSIVE PREP SCRIMMAGE

We run a defensive scrimmage on Monday and Tuesday if we play on Friday. The period is usually twenty-six minutes in length and we run nearly forty plays in that time frame. Before Monday's practice, a scout offensive squad is listed on the bulletin board. We use third stringers on this squad because we scrimmage both first and second unit defenses against the opponent plays. At the beginning of the period, the scout squad is assembled and the coach in charge gets a play card from the manager (Diagram 13-9) who yells out the yard line, down and distance, and hash mark to the

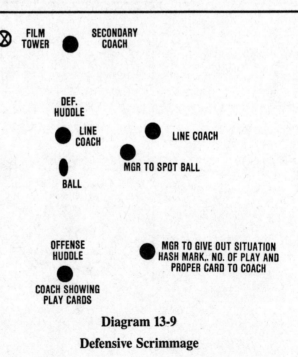

Diagram 13-9

Defensive Scrimmage

defense. A second manager spots the ball at the proper position, while the defensive coaches huddle their unit. Each coach has a copy of the ready list. The defensive signal caller is assisted in his call by the defensive coaches. As the drill progresses through the second day, the signal callers should become more independent in making the calls. Automatics according to formation distortion are often built into the game plan. We sometimes start the drill on Monday by running at full contact without tackling, and progress to full scrimmage about halfway through Monday's work.

On Tuesday we want to full scrimmage for the entire drill. We run the first unit two-thirds of the time and the second unit one-third of the time. When we complete the twenty-six plays on the ready list, we start again with the first play listed and continue until we have no more scheduled time. The drill is recorded from behind the defense. Evaluation of the videotape or film tells us immediately what assignment and technique errors must be corrected.

DEFENSIVE RECOGNITION DRILL

We would like to use this drill every week, but we only have time when there is a Saturday game. If this is the case, we run this drill on Monday for a period of sixteen minutes. The idea is to adjust to opponent formations and field positions (Diagram 13-10) without running any plays. We show only formations on the cards and the scout squad hurries out of the huddle to align in position to permit the defense to do likewise. A manager handles the play cards in conjunction with the scout squad coach while another manager spots the ball. Coaches make corrections and discuss technique with their positions. This is an excellent way to get a jump on the game plan.

GAME-TESTED DEFENSIVE BREAKAWAY DRILL

Employment of our method of defensive prep scrimmage does not allow us to practice pursuit against long runs. It took us one season of play in which we did a good job in all defensive phases (with the exception of giving up several long touchdown runs) to recognize that we needed to program a drill that would give us the desired practice. The scout squad seldom breaks away for long runs, so every Tuesday (for a Friday game) we draw up four breakaway plays and take at least two defenders out of the defensive unit for

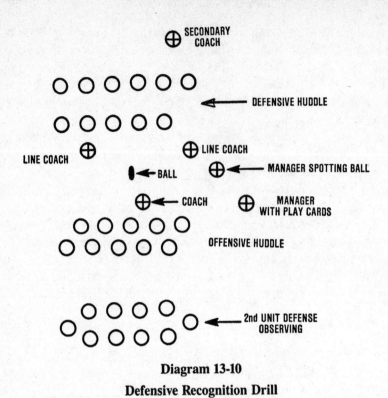

Diagram 13-10
Defensive Recognition Drill

each play (Diagram 13-11). The plays are live and they are opponent plays, except we use blockers who would be blocking the "dead" players to lead interference or block other positions. The setup for this drill is the same as for the ready list defensive prep scrimmage. Do not neglect this drill; it will pay dividends. We use it in the second week of practice in the pre-season at the conclusion of our ready list period.

GAME-TESTED GOAL LINE DEFENSE SESSION

We scrimmage goal line defense against the scout squad two days before the game. We allow eight minutes for this period and draw up eight plays just as we expect the opponent to run them against our goal line defense. We can repeat any plays that we do not defend well (Diagram 13-12). The managers and coaches are set up just as they are for the defensive prep period, and we record the

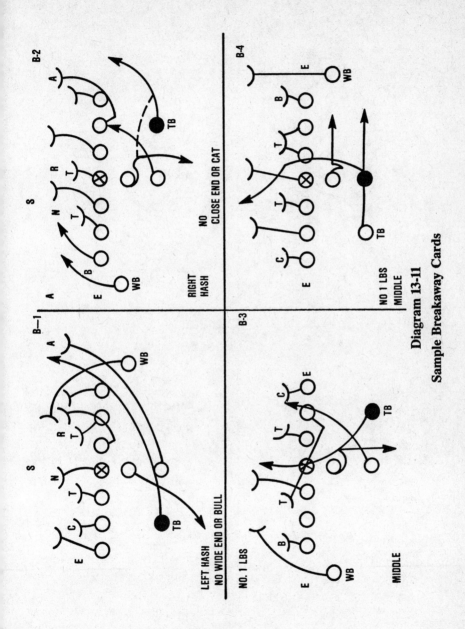

Diagram 13-11
Sample Breakaway Cards

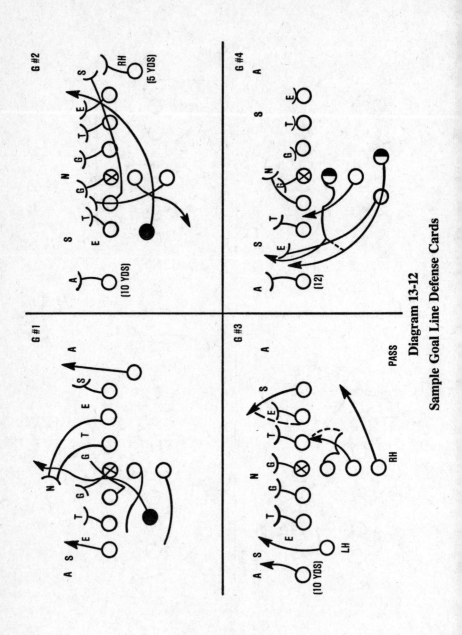

Diagram 13-12

Sample Goal Line Defense Cards

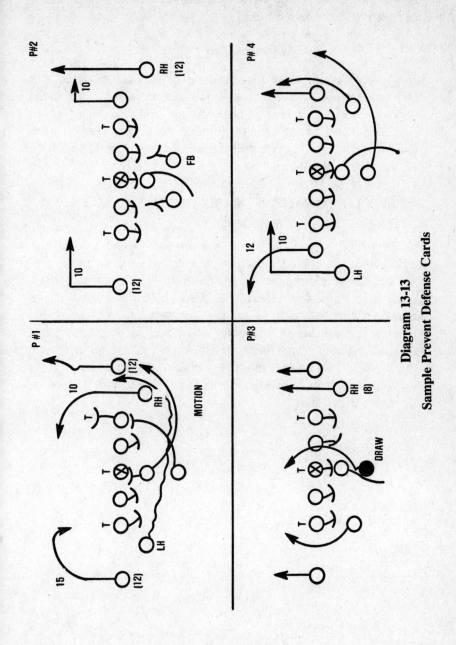

Diagram 13-13
Sample Prevent Defense Cards

action. In the pre-season we work goal line defense four times for periods of fifteen minutes each.

PREVENT DEFENSE

On cards we draw two or three plays that we expect our opponents to use when they are behind late in the half or late in the game against our prevent defense. We set up the drill just as we would the ready list and use a two-minute period two days before the game (Diagram 13-13). We drill it once during the pre-season for a period of fifteen minutes.

SPECIAL SITUATIONS—GAME-TESTED PREPARATION

We do not have time to break down into special defensive situations, but if you completely platoon players and coaches it is advisable to do this once each week and at least twice in the pre-season. Script and draw cards for the following situations: (1) two minutes defense when ahead; (2) desperation defense when you must get the ball away from the opponent; (3) defensing the opponent inside his own twenty yard line; (4) defenses against unusual plays and formations which the opponent has run anytime in the past few seasons, and (5) complete surprise situations—practicing application of adjustments to possible unexpected formations or "trick" plays.

FOURTEEN

Action-Tested Drills for Specialists

It is easy to pay lip service to the specialists. Kickers, kick blockers, return men, and long snappers do not learn their craft by accident. It is through intensive drill that such players are developed. The fundamentals necessary for good specialty play must be taught and practiced with the same meticulous approach as the fundamentals for the other phases of football.

GAME-TESTED PUNTER DRILLS

The punters line up in stances on a chalk mark. The knees are slightly flexed, feet about twelve inches apart with the right foot in advance of the left foot in a heel and toe relationship (the left foot is forward if the punter is left footed). The coach has the punters take a short step with the lead foot and then a long step with the left foot, then carry out the kicking motion with the kicking foot by smoothly swinging the leg and extending the toes. This is a one-time-only drill, done on the first day of practice.

With the same alignment, the punters go through the steps and drop the football, checking the drop. The ball is held (for the right

207

footed punter) with the left hand underneath the ball so that the fingers are across the bottom seam with the thumb across the left seam. It is gripped lightly by the left hand, with the hand placed slightly forward of the midsection of the ball. The right hand is placed behind the midsection of the ball so that the thumb runs across the rear of the laces and the fingers cross the right seam. To execute the drop, the punter extends his hands so that the elbows are relatively straight at belt level, and drops the ball when the left foot strikes the ground on the second step. He does not kick the ball, but checks the drop to insure that it is a good one. When the ball strikes the ground it should bounce slightly backward and to the right. That will occur if the front point of the ball is depressed and slightly to the left at the time of the drop. We repeat this process about fifteen times. It is a drill we do every day in the first week of pre-season drills, then we discontinue it unless we ascertain that the punter is making a bad drop later in the season.

Using punters facing each other in groups of two and positioning them ten yards apart on chalk marks, they go through the kicking steps and actually place the ball on the instep of the kicking foot and punch it ten yards to their partners. This is an excellent drill for keeping the eye on the football, practicing the proper drop, and making good contact with the ball. Each punter gets ten punches. We do this drill in the first week of practice, then discontinue unless we feel that the punter is having ball "contact" troubles later in the season. The punters line up on a chalk mark and punt the ball with the normal kicking motion. There is a group of return men located downfield and the punters take turns while the coach makes corrections. We do this drill the first two days of practice before the punters are working with centers, then we seldom take a regular punt without a center. Each punter gets ten punts.

We like to have the punters work with centers from the third day of practice until the end of the season. There are two sets of return men and at least two punters working with two centers simultaneously. Reserve punters wait their turn. Managers shag balls and coaches make corrections (Diagram 14-1). We like to have each punter get ten kicks each day. We do not use a stop watch to time the punter's rhythm as we feel it is more important to establish the proper steps; then the time will take care of itself.

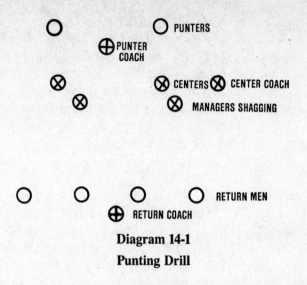

Diagram 14-1

Punting Drill

Three long steps are no advantage over a two-step kicking rhythm, and the three steps invite the blocked punt. Often the three-step punter has to hurry and shorten his stride when rushed, resulting in a badly shanked punt, something we see a lot of in modern football. We occasionally clock the punter's hang time in order to point out to him the necessity of the high kick for effective coverage. It is in the summer months that the varsity punter is developed. We ask the punters to kick up to a hundred times each day in the summer after the kicking leg is in shape. It cannot be emphasized too much that a good punter is consistent in his application of the fundamentals, causing his results to be consistently good. Punters should practice in all kinds of weather conditions, both with and against the wind.

Out of bounds kicking can be an important adjunct to your team's effectiveness. Our statistics reflect that we have a better chance of scoring than the opposition when they are backed up inside their own ten yard line. If your punting game can effectively put them out of bounds inside the ten when you have fourth down from their forty to their twenty-five, you will have accrued a tremendous advantage. Nevertheless, do not delude yourself into trying to kick out of bounds without the proper amount and quality of practice by the punter and by the punting team against pressure.

The punters practice out of bounds kicks from different lateral positions. Align the punters with a center and place the ball on the right hash. A "shagger" is located on the five yard line where it intersects with the boundary, and markers are placed down at boundary intersections on the ten yard line and at the goal line. The punter aims the ball for the shagger. An evaluation of the success of the punt can be made right away. The punter tries to kick out to the right for the right hash and middle field positions and to the left for left hash positions. We take six out of bounds kicks every day in the specialty periods.

It is beneficial to drill for the bad snap. The kicker is aligned without a center and the coach rolls a ball to the punter or throws it over his head. The punter chases the ball, retrieves it and kicks it on the run. After a few times with this action, add a rusher so the punter can elude him and then kick on the run. We do this drill once in pre-season and three or four times in season.

LONG SNAPPER DRILLS

This is the most neglected fundamental in the game. The bad snap results in not getting the kick off, getting the kick blocked, and the poor kick. We teach at least six players to long snap for punts and placements every year. There is no excuse to get caught short of long snappers. Our method of teaching the long snap enables us to teach about one-third of our players to execute an effective long snap. Other methods have not been nearly as successful for us.

We align the long snappers on a chalk mark and have a coach demonstrate the passer's grip on the ball for the right-handed centers. The centers place the ball over the head with the laces up and the other hand placed on the bottom of the ball with the middle finger running along the bottom seam. The centers then separate in groups of two, five yards apart, and commence throwing the ball back and forth to each other. The emphasis is on thrusting the elbows forward for a slingshot effect and following through by giving the wrists a hard rotation, forcing the plams outward. We do this drill every day as a warm-up for the long snappers. In the early part of the pre-season, they take ten passes each; as the season progresses, three or four passes is sufficient.

The next step in the teaching progression for the long snap is to have the centers turn their backs to each other at a distance of six or seven yards and hold the ball off the ground a distance of one foot with the same grip with the laces down, the eyes looking through the legs and focused on the receiver's belt buckle. The feet are about shoulder width and even. Contrary to many coaches, we believe it is possible to have too wide a stance for the long snapper. The ball is extended and the center thrusts the arms backward with the slingshot effect, following through by turning the palms outward. If the follow-through is correct, the ball will arrive on target. If the center takes either hand off the ball early, the ball will torque and go off target. If the palms go up rather than out the ball is likely to elevate and go over the punter's head.

In this coaching phase, we show the centers how to slide. When the hands thrust through the legs, the feet slide backwards a few inches, supplying a little more momentum to the snap of the ball. We get ten snaps each the first few days of pre-season practice. As the season goes on, the better snappers only do this drill two or three times. The inexperienced or "shaky" snappers continue to do ten of these every day until we feel progress warrants cutting down on this drill.

We like to line the centers up side by side on a chalk mark and have them "shadow box" the long snap without a football. The center extends his hands slightly in front of the head and holds the imaginary ball approximately one foot off the ground. The eyes are looking through the legs and focused on the coach. Each center dummies as the coach calls his name. The elbows are thrust through the legs in slingshot fashion, the palms are thrust outward hard, and the center slides backward on the snap. Each center gets four thrusts and is encouraged to make each thrust as hard as he can. We do this drill only in the first week of pre-season practice.

We put the center with the punter on the third day of pre-season practice. We have the center hold the ball and the kicker is positioned twelve yards behind the ball. The centers are coached to make the snap by using the thrust of the elbows, following through with the plams out, and by using the slide. The drill is organized so that the first string center gets at least six snaps with the first punter and the alternates get six snaps with each other, then we mix the alternates with the regulars for about four snaps (Diagram 14-2). We

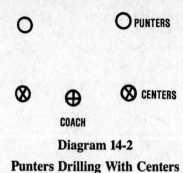

Diagram 14-2

Punters Drilling With Centers

do not have the centers place the ball on the ground until the second week of pre-season practice.

When we work from the ground, the center gets his grip on the ball and places no weight on the ball. The snap is executed as previously described. We have the center place the ball down on the ground to simulate the official's spot, walk back toward the ball and get over it, adjust it, and execute the snap. An experienced center who has good upper body strength may eliminate the slide; we do this with discretion.

The snap for the placement is executed just as the snap for the punt, except the center must be careful not to get too much on the ball; it must be a softer pass. The centers are rotated so that the first center works with the first holder and kicker, the second unit works together, and the alternates get a few snaps with the regulars and vice-versa. We do this for both extra points and field goals (Diagram 14-3).

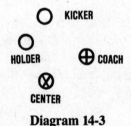

Diagram 14-3

Centers With Holders and Place Kickers

GAME-TESTED PUNT BLOCK DRILLS

A blocked punt often turns a game around. Teams that do a good job blocking punts do not do so by accident; it is a skill that can be taught and drilled. Unfortunately, few coaches take the time or trouble to work on the fundamentals of blocking punts. I belonged in that category for many years.

Members of the punt block unit are aligned just behind a chalk stripe in the relative positions they would be in for a punting situation. A gym mat is placed at a spot where the punt is expected to be made. For the twelve-yard punter who is right-footed, we feel the point is about nine yards deep and one foot to the left of the punter. A marker is placed down at the spot where the ball connects with the foot and another marker is placed down where the punter would be initially aligned (Diagram 14-4).

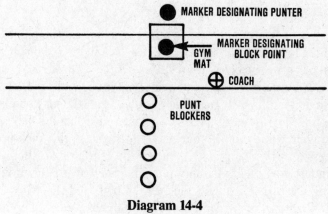

Diagram 14-4

Punt Block Extension Drill

The blockers are given instructions by the coach as to the technique of the punt block. A fast take-off is a necessity. The blockers use two- or four-point stances, but must not false step in starting. All the weight must be concentrated on the push-off foot. The blocker must drive hard for the spot of the kick and aim his extension for the point of the kick so that his face will be on the kicker's foot. If the charge angle is wrong, he could rough the punter. A full extension or dive is made by thrusting off either foot (players must *not* slow up, collect, and take off from both feet) and making the body parallel to the ground. The blocker must accelerate all the way up to the extension. He extends the arms fully and crosses the wrists. Each blocker gets four attempts on the third and fifth day of pre-season practice, then we discontinue the drill.

In the second week of pre-season practice, we add a punter to the drill and then continue it every other day for the rest of the pre-season and carry out the drill once each week during the season. We do not use a first or second string punter for the drill. In the pre-season, our punter goes through his normal steps and kicking rhythm from his standard distance. During the season, we use opponent films to coach our punter to simulate the opponents' depth and steps. Each blocker gets two attempts at the punt. We have the coach allow the blocker to begin his charge, then signal the punter when to begin the punting motion. This drill is a *must* if you plan to block punts.

I have had teams block punts and fail to capitalize on the resulting loose ball. We have a drill for picking up the blocked kicks and it has given us better results. First, if the kick is blocked and the ball is behind the line of scrimmage, not in the end zone, and it is a fourth down play, we insist that our defender attempt to pick up the ball and run with it. Emphasize to your squad that the ball will still be in your possession if your player mishandles this pick-up, since possession will change as a result of the fourth down situation. We begin teaching this by simply bouncing the ball on the ground and having the rusher redirect, pick up the ball, and run with it.

We progress this skill by aligning three rushers to go after the loose ball, but putting a surrogate punter into the action (who must be blocked by one of the rushers who does not get to the ball). It is amazing how many punters make touchdown saving tackles on players running with a previously blocked punt. A bit of drill work on this phase can go a long way.

We do the loose ball punt block drills twice in the pre-season and three or four times during the season. Additionally, in the regular individual punt block drills, we have the defender who successfully carries out the block get up and pick up the loose ball and run with it.

PLACEMENT BLOCK DRILLS

In blocking placements, a mat is set up with a marker seven yards behind the chalk stripe. Another marker series allows the two outside blockers to align properly for the block. The inside man runs a straight line (inside the wing) and gets a good start without false stepping, thrusts off the fourth step to extend so that the body is parallel to the ground and the face is on the ball. The outside man steps at an angle over the face of the wing's original position for two steps, plants the outside foot and drives straight for the marker, extending off the second step after the plant, driving for a flat extension with the face on the ball (Diagram 14-5). The theory is that if the wing blocks to the inside, the outside man will be free; if the wing takes the outside, the inside man will be free. This drill is done three times in the pre-season and once a week during the season. Each of the blockers makes three attempts.

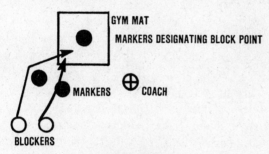

Diagram 14-5

Placement Block Extension Drill

GAME-TESTED PLACE KICKER'S DRILLS

Place kick candidates line up on a chalk mark and the coach faces them and puts them in the proper stance. Stances vary as to soccer style or conventional style, left-footed or right-footed. The coach talks them through the steps and then has them dummy through the kicking procedure. On the first day of practice they get twenty dummy kicks each. The drill is discontinued after that.

Next, the place kickers learn to work with a kickoff tee, but only with two-step movement. The kickers are aligned; the tees are placed on the ground; the ball is set and they go through a two-step kick while the coach watches and makes corrections. Each player gets ten kicks for the drill. We continue this drill only for the first three days of pre-season practice.

We have the place kickers begin work with a center and holder on the fourth day of pre-season practice. The three-man team goes through an extra point routine with a shagger beyond the goal post. The first group works together most, but alternates must be inserted so that all holders, kickers, and centers get an opportunity to do some work together. The first two kickers should get five extra points each practice. We also attempt field goals at various depths and at various lateral field positions. If a chart is kept of each kicker's efficiency (Diagram 14-6), it is a handy guide in planning field goal attempts during a game. As an example, if a kicker is weak at certain distances from the left hash, the coach may be better advised to run a scrimmage play or an out of bounds punt in that particular situation.

Name	Yard Line	Hash	Attempts	Good
Jones	Extra Point	————————	10	9
	15	Left	4	2
	20	Right	4	4
	25	Left	3	1
	30	Right	3	2
	35	Left	3	0
	35	Middle	3	1
	40	Right	2	0
Murhile	Extra Point	————————	5	5
	15	Left	3	2
	20	Middle	3	3
	25	Right	3	1
	30	Right	3	0
	35	Middle	3	2
	40	Left	3	1

Diagram 14-6: Placement Effectiveness Chart

In teaching the kick-off, the motion is exactly the same as for the placement, except the kicker is allowed more steps in order to establish more momentum. It is up to the coach to work out the steps with the kicker. We usually start with four steps and let the kicker do his kick-offs with four steps for the first week of practice. We then progress to more steps under the guidance of the coach. It is my observation that kick-off men tend to take too many steps rather than not enough; if we feel that the kicker cannot time his steps, we insist that he go back to four steps for a few days until we again want to try additional steps. We have had some fine kickers who used four steps.

Kick-off men work in two's and get at opposite ends of the field, each with a kicking tee and a ball. Each tees up a ball at his location. The approach is made and the first man carries out his kick. Immediately afterwards, the second kicker carries out his kick-off. Each kicker retrieves the ball at his own end, tees up the ball, and kicks again (Diagram 14-7).

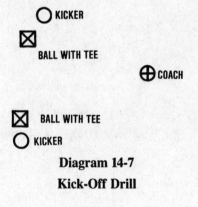

Diagram 14-7

Kick-Off Drill

Late in the second week of pre-season practice, we have our kick-off men get ten yards apart and try a few onside kicks. If we target the top of the ball, we can develop a good onside kick. We take about two or three onside kicks each week in-season.

As in punting, place kickers develop themselves in the off-season. A dedicated place kicker will get his leg in good enough condition to make one hundred kicks each day in the summer months.

GAME-TESTED PUNT RETURNERS' DRILLS

Punt returners are usually arranged in teams of two or three. We arrange return candidates into groups of two and have the coach instruct them as to how the kicks will be called and the fundamentals of receiving punts. The punt returner is taught to catch the punt by tucking the elbows in at the bottom of the rib cage and extending the arms with the palms up. The receiver jockeys under the punt and catches the ball in the "basket," bending at the waist slightly and bringing the right knee up softly to cushion the ball. We have our receiving teams arranged so that there is a front man and a back man. The back man is the "call" man and his calls to the up man are "yours," "fair catch," "mine," or "get away." After these instructions, the coach throws a few high passes and has the returners receive the ball properly while making the proper calls (Diagram 14-8). When the back man deems that the ball is not playable, both

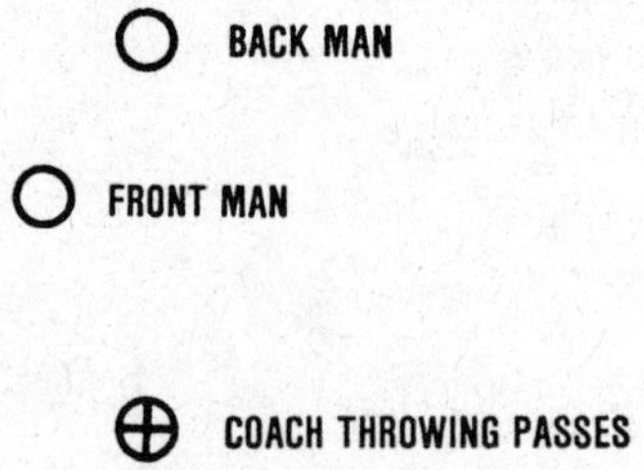

O   BACK MAN

O   FRONT MAN

⊕   COACH THROWING PASSES

Diagram 14-8

Punt Returner Drill Using Passes

he and his partner should backpedal away from it, keeping the eyes focused on it at all times. It is emphasized to the return groups that they must attempt to field all punts on the fly, that only a predictable first bounce may be fielded, and that a ball is not fielded after that predictable first bounce. We have the coach throw the ball to the return men for the first three days of pre-season practice, then we work with the punters (Diagram 14-9). We do the drill every day. Twice during the pre-season and every other week during the season we have the return group work on fielding punts inside the ten yard line. We ask the call man to use his judgement on calling for the reception of punts inside the ten, since they may bounce into the end

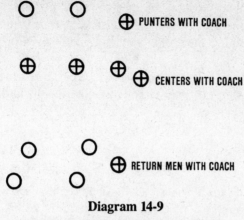

Diagram 14-9

Punt Returner Drill With Punters

zone if the coverage is not close. We ask the call man not to field any punts inside the five yard line.

If you anticipate playing against a left-footed punter, the return men should see a lot of left-footed punts that particular week, since the spiral is opposite. If you cannot find a left-footed punter to work against, left-handed passes can be substituted.

KICK-OFF RETURNERS' DRILLS

Kick-off return men are placed in proper relative positions on the return alignment and instructed as to the rules for the free kick

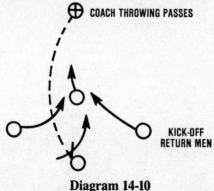

Diagram 14-10

Backs Working Kick-Off Return Maneuver

and the touchback. Passes are thrown to each of the backs and the backs go through the return maneuver (Diagram 14-10), whether it be wedge, assigned men, or any other maneuver. This particular drill is done late in the first week of pre-season practice, then repeated with a kicker late in the second week of pre-season practice. During the season, kick-off return men do not do this drill as part of individual specialties; instead they take two or three kicks after each practice in order to stay sharp on receiving kicks.

TEACHING DRILL FOR PLACEMENT HOLDERS

This is a one-time-only drill, since the holders work with the centers and kickers after the initial instruction period. The holders are aligned on a chalk mark beside a placement tee. The coach instructs the holder to place the left knee down beside the tee and extend the right leg (for the right-footed kicker). He extends his hands and the coach tosses him an underhand spiral pass which he receives and places down on the tee with the left hand on top of the ball.

If you overlook the kicking game fundamentals, you will eventually pay the price on the scoreboard. The hidden yardage in the kicking game and the morale factor involved in it must not be underestimated.

FIFTEEN

Drills for Special Teams

It was not until I did a thorough statistical analysis of yardage, field position, and drive continuity that I fully realized the importance of the kicking game. You will find that the kicking game plays comprise about 20% of the total plays for a season. The great majority of kicking plays involve large quantities of yardage, scoring, ball exchange, or a combination of these factors. Analyze your films and see how much yardage and how many critical situations are involved in the kicking game, and I am sure that you will rethink the care and planning that you give the kicking game.

The special teams provide a unique opportunity for you to improve overall squad performance and team morale. You can generously platoon and make use of many different kinds of talent in all phases of the kicking game. If the coaching staff sets the proper emphasis, the reaction of your squad will be beneficial.

We assign primary and back-up units for each unit of special team play and post these squad lists on the bulletin board in addition to dummy special team units to work against. We take copies of these lists on the field so there is never confusion in regard to special team personnel.

GAME-TESTED DRILLS FOR THE PUNTING TEAM

Early in pre-season practice, we introduce the punts and punt returns in a special mid-day practice that lasts less than one hour and constitutes a teaching session. We think that this allows us to cover our introductory on-the- field instruction at a slow and relaxed pace. The players are given their assignments prior to taking the field and, after stretching, the front line is aligned in punt formation while punters and long snappers are warming up and deep blockers are being given blocking assignments and coverage patterns. The deep backs (Diagram 15-1) are set up to take the blocks of rushers with shields and the front line, without centers, is walked through coverage patterns from both hashes and the middle of the field (Diagram 15-2).

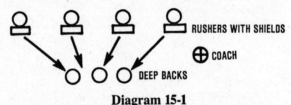

Diagram 15-1

Deep Backs Working Against Shield Rush

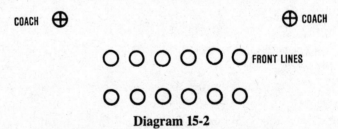

Diagram 15-2

Walking Front Lines Through Coverage Patterns

It is very important to emphasize the proper fan in this drill period. Our fan rules are: (1) ends, halfway from the spotted position of the ball to the sideline, (2) tackles, five yards inside the end fan routes, (3) guards, ten yards inside the end fan routes. We want the fan routes to be achieved by the time the coverage has progressed ten yards upfield (Diagram 15-3). After two walk-thrus from all positions for all units, we bring all components of the punting team together and align them against air.

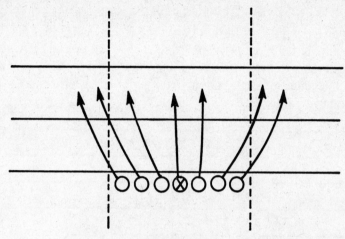

Diagram 15-3

Fan Routes From Middle for Front Line

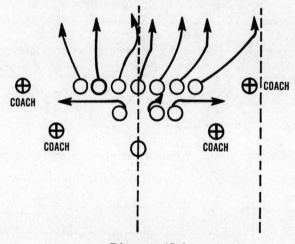

Diagram 15-4

Whistle After Quick Fan Routes

We have the punt team huddle, break, and align over the ball properly. The punter signals the center with his hands when the team is set and he is ready. The center snaps the ball when he is ready after the signal. The coverage unit does not release until the coach signals a short blast with the whistle; then they sprint into the coverage routes and try to stop quickly when the coach lets go with a long blast on the whistle (Diagram 15-4). The coach wants to get the front line into the fan routes. The blockers in the back line and the punter start for their coverage routes when the ball is kicked. We go through this procedure for each punting team twice from left, middle, and right hash marks.

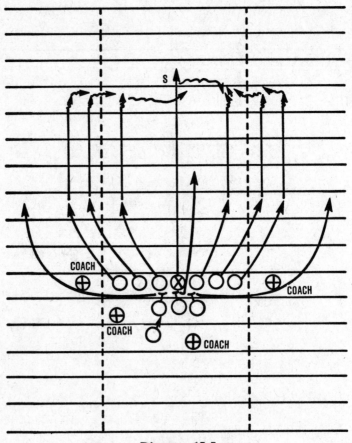

Diagram 15-5

Coverage Closing Ball Carrier

In the next phase, we use almost the same procedure, except we have the coverage units go through the entire coverage and close the ball carrier after the slight whistle delay by the coach (Diagram 15-5). Our center drives hard for the ball carrier and does not attempt to slow down or come under control. The concept is to try and make the safety delay his progress by forcing him to delay and dodge the center. If the center should make quick contact with the safety, he may jar the ball loose. In cases where the fair catch is signaled, the center runs past the safety as close as he can, which should add a distraction factor. The rest of the coverage closes the ball by depressing the hips and coming under control about five yards from the depth of the ball. The players on the front line of the coverage unit want to draw a bead on the outside numeral of the safety. We will not tackle the safety in this particular drill, but we have him catch the ball and zigzag, which means the people in the coverage pattern break down and shuffle with shoulders square in pursuit of the ball (Diagram 15-6). We have the coverage units use this procedure twice from left, middle, and right hashes.

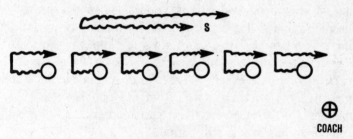

Diagram 15-6
Front Line Shuffling and Closing Safety

In the final teaching phase of the punt team drills, we line up a defensive team and go through the blocking rules on the line. We then go through the entire procedure of break, alignment, block, punt, and cover except we do not tackle the safety. We use this drill once from each field position against a different defensive alignment each time. The defenders rush the punter so we get used to kicking pressure (Diagram 15-7).

After the initial coaching session, we practice all our punting

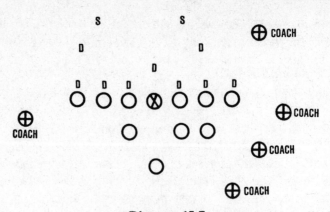

Diagram 15-7
Team Punt Drill Versus Defense

team situations at the end of practice in the pre-season and during the season. We use punt team drills every other day in the pre-season and once each week during the season. If we have a Saturday game, we drill the punting team twice, on Monday and again on Wednesday. For Friday games, we cover this work on Tuesday. We try many kinds of alignments and returns against our punt team in the pre-season. For this drill, we usually go live without tackling, although I think it is necessary to add tackling a few times in pre-season and once every few weeks in the season. In-season, we use the scouting report to determine exactly what kind of alignment, pressure, and return patterns we can expect from the opponents and in what situations we can look for these particular patterns. We simulate these conditions in our drill period.

It is necessary to kick under pressure from deep in your own territory. As a result, we devote two punting sessions in the pre-season to working punts from inside the five yard line from all hash positions. Make sure the punter understands the rules for scoring a safety. In particular, he must know that he must not step on the end line. There are situations in which the punter may determine that it is better to accept a safety in the end zone than to have the punt blocked for a possible touchdown. If you send your punter into the game on the fourth down, you can tell him, based on score, time remaining, and other factors, when to make such a play. You need to do a lot of blackboard work with your punter to enable him to cope with the intricacies of possible critical situations. During the season, we practice two or three punts from inside the five yard line every third week.

There are times when you may want to take a deliberate safety. Although such situations are relatively rare, we do not want any confusion to exist when we decide to carry out this maneuver. It is not enough to go over this procedure on the blackboard or to simply give instructions to the punter. I have seen teams misinterpret a coach's instructions and wind up giving up an easy touchdown, thus losing the game. We go through the deliberate safety situation once in the pre-season.

We have the punter take the snap, move for the far corner of the end zone, and step out of the end zone when he is about to be tackled. The idea is to use up as much time as possible and take the safety. The punt team and especially the punter must understand that they cannot lose possession of the ball in the end zone, and that they must not advance the ball beyond the goal line on fourth down.

Most teams have a fake punt play or two in their repertoire, and it is necessary to practice such a play as part of the punting period. How much you practice these "gadgets" depends on how much you plan to use them. For us, a couple of times in the pre-season is good, and in most cases, once every three or four weeks during the season will suffice. There are certain instances in which the scouting report tells us that the possibilities of successful fake punts are particularly high in certain situations. Consequently, we give the fake punts more emphasis in those weeks.

It is also a good idea to work on kicking out of bounds to pin the opponents deep in their own territory. We do this at the end of all punt periods and use one punt from each hash against the opponents' expected rush and coverage pattern. I had to learn the hard way that the punter must work against pressure to perfect the out of bounds kick. Just practicing it against air will not get the job done.

GAME-TESTED PUNT RETURN TEAM DRILLS

Once again, get out those game films. Go over all your punt return situations. Check how many times your opponents' coverage was poor—there is a potential long return each time. If the snap, kicking rhythm, or protection was poor, there is a potential blocked punt. Take advantage of this phase of the game. You won't be sorry.

We use part of the first midday teaching session in the pre-season to introduce the punt return. We take our punt return squad and line them up against a dummy punt unit, going through the assignments, and walking through punt return patterns (Diagram 15-8). I believe that two or three well-executed patterns are enough. After the walk through, the return people work against the punt team full speed, except there is no tackling. The ball is positioned from left, middle, and right hash marks. We take six returns for primary and back-up units.

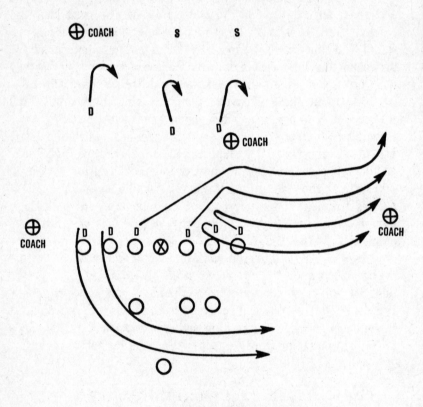

Diagram 15-8
Walking Through Punt Return Assignments

In the second week of pre-season practice, we work on punt
block schemes (Diagram 15-9). We align in the regular punt return
setup and have one side of the defense execute a punt return in that
direction, while the other side attempts to block the punt. We do not
turn loose both sides at once; we want to avoid collision injuries. In
the pre-season, we work punt returns every other day. We attempt a
return from left, middle,and right hash, and we also attempt to block
two or three punts. Once or twice in the pre-season, we attempt to
turn loose our entire front line and block the punt. It is also
necessary to have a delayed return pattern for these cases in which
your squad attempts to block the punt and does not make it. Most
coaches set up a return wall on a pre-designated side in such
situations.

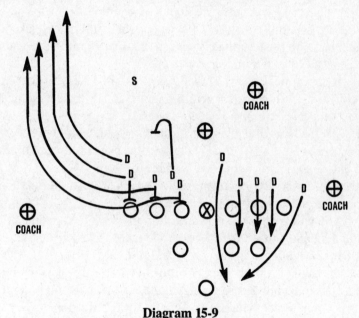

Diagram 15-9
Punt Block—Half Line Return Drill

During the season, we use our scouting report to determine
whether we will try to return the punts in a certain way or whether
we will try to block the punts according to the situation. There have

been weeks in which we have tried to block all opponent punts and other weeks in which we try to return them all. Generally, we work for a pattern in which there are some returns and some blocks. We want to set up a "return game plan" in which we return wide side, short side, or middle in certain field positions, or block the kick in some specific cases. In designing the block, we sometimes execute the scheme from our regular return alignment, or we may design a special punt block alignment which can include up to ten men to block the punt. In these designs, we want to take advantage of opponent weaknesses in protecting the punter or the excessive length of time taken by the opponent in the execution of the punt.

There are defensive situations in which the opponent may quick kick against you. About twice in the pre-season, we have the team punt in a defensive scrimmage. We designate a wall to a certain side if a quick kick occurs. We do not review this during the season unless the scouting report tells us the opponent has quick kicked, in which case we try to imitate their quick kick in scrimmage and set up our wall after the punt is executed.

It is also necessary to practice against the fake punt with your return team. A sound punt return has provisions for defending the fake punt. Nevertheless, unless you take some time to practice against the "surprise fake punt" on the field, you stand a good possibility of getting "burnt." We work this play a couple of times in the pre-season and about every three or four weeks during the season. If a scouted opponent indicates a fake punt, we definitely practice against it during game week.

You will find yourself in situations in which the opponent lines up to punt and you are very wary of the fake; you may want to leave your regular defense in the game and drop a single safety back to field the punt. If that is the case, practice this once or twice in the pre-season, having a designated side to wall if it should be a punt. Practice against both fakes and punts in this situation. Cover this once or twice during the regular season.

There are also desperation situations in which you are certain that a fake punt is imminent and in which you do not wish to handle the ball. We use our base defense here and cover this only one time in the pre-season.

GAME-TESTED KICK-OFF TEAM DRILLS

If your squad kicks-off a great deal, you are probably winning. However, it seems a terrible waste to work hard and earn a score, to have the opponent set himself up in good field position by virtue of your poor kick-off coverage. In our kick-off scheme, we may kick the ball from either hash or from the middle of the field. In a particular game we choose only one or two field positions to use as kick-off launching points.

We teach kick-off coverage in a special midday session late in the first week of pre-season practice. We align the kick-off team,

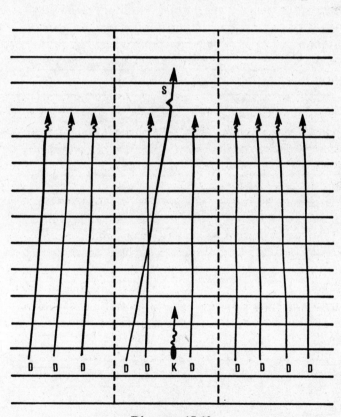

Diagram 15-10
Kick-Off Coverage Versus Air

paying particular attention to proper spacing. One safety is upfield to receive the ball. The kick-off team sprints down the field and closes the return man by getting the hips down and coming under control about five yards before arriving at the safety's depth, and shuffles to draw a bead on the return man's outside numeral (Diagram 15-10). We have one player who is designated to drive upfield without coming under control. His function is merely to make the safety delay and force our man to miss him. After about three coverages by each kick-off unit, we put up a dummy unit and have them attempt a kick-off return against our kick-off team. Each unit gets two of these kick-offs (Diagram 15-11). We do not tackle in this drill.

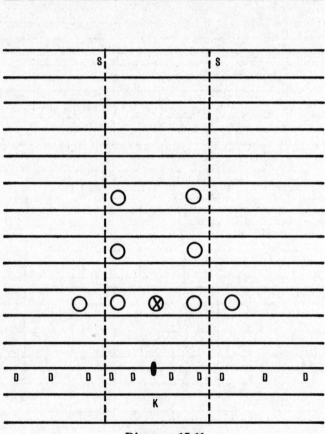

Diagram 15-11

Kick-Off Cover Vs. Return

After installing the kick-offs, we work on them at the end of practice in the pre-season. Each unit gets four or five kick-offs. We tackle in one of these sessions late in the second week of pre-season practice. We work kick-offs once each week during the season, with each unit again getting four or five coverages. We do not tackle in this drill (although the blocking is live) unless we feel that our kick-off unit was deficient in tackling the previous week.

There are two distinct situations in which you may wish to employ the onside kick-off. In the first case, the scouting report may tell you that your opponents are aligned or react in such a manner that the onside kick would be a good gamble. In the second case, you may find yourself at a point where you are kicking off and are in desperate need of possession of the ball. Of course, the quality of your onside kick-off man will have a lot to do with how often you use the maneuver. In addition, if you have a poor deep kick-off man, it may be a good gamble to kick onside more often. We use the onside scheme (Diagram 15-12) as part of the kick-off drill several times during the pre-season and practice it about every other week during the season. If we plan to use the onside kick as a surprise weapon, we will practice it three or four times in that particular week.

There are times in which you wish to kick the ball short and on the ground to prevent any possibility of the long return. These are

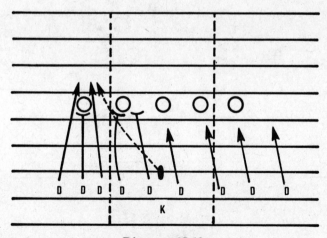

Diagram 15-12
Onside Kick-Off Scheme

nearly always late-in-the-game protect-your-lead cases. We work on these kicks three or four times in the pre-season and about once every three weeks during the season.

GAME-TESTED KICK-OFF RETURN DRILLS

If you are receiving a lot of kick-offs you are probably losing a lot, so we do not emphasize this phase of the kicking game as much as the others. Nevertheless, I think it is necessary to do well enough with kick-off returns to start your offensive drive in good field position. Also, the morale factor involved in the long and touchdown returns cannot be overlooked.

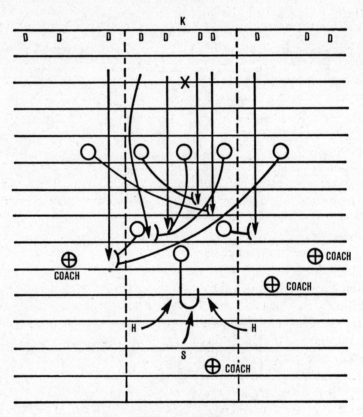

Diagram 15-13

Grabbing Assigned Men for Kick-Off Return

We introduce the kick-off return in the second midday session held at the end of the first week of pre-season practice. We set up our return team and a dummy kick-off team. Coaches are placed so they can coach their positions. The ball is kicked deep, and the return team assumes its pattern. For this teaching drill, the blockers grab the coverage men, stopping their progress at that point, allowing the return to continue upfield (Diagram 15-13). This method allows us to determine and get to our assignments, helps us to gain our timing, and gets the backs into the proper return channel. Each return unit gets three shots for each return on this drill. One or two kick-off return patterns is all we use. In subsequent pre-season practices, we work on kick-off returns every other day for a period of about five or six minutes. In those sessions, we return and block live, except for tackling (Diagram 15-14). We tackle on this drill only about once or twice in the pre-season. We work on kick-off returns once each week during the season. We set up the dummy kick-off team so that it is a facsimle of the opponent's squad, with the proper positions assumed for ball placement, safety, kicker, coverage routes, and so on. We may want to make slight adjustments in the return pattern to take advantage of any weaknesses in the coverage scheme of the opponents.

It is important that members of the kick-off return team thoroughly understand the rules governing this phase of the game. It is imperative that you emphasize: (1) all blocking must be above the waist, (2) a kick-off traveling ten yards is free once it strikes the ground or one of our players, (3) it is possible to fair catch a kick-off, (4) a kick breaking the plane of the goal line is a touchback and cannot be played, and (5) a ball driven by the impetus of the kick, even if muffed or touched by the receiving team, is still a touchback if it rolls into the end zone. They must also understand that a kick-off that goes out of bounds allows the receiving team to put the ball in play at a favorable field position. You need only to watch a kick return man backing away from a free ball as if it were a scrimmage kick to realize the importance of knowing the rules.

It is necessary to work against the inadvertant short kick and the unexpected onside kick. We work on this twice during the pre-season and occasionally during the season (more often if we are facing a kick-off man who is skilled on the onside kick). We want

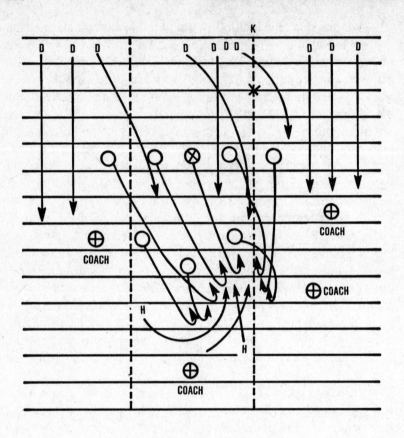

Diagram 15-14

Kick-Off Return Drill (No Tackling)

our front line to get possession of the ball on the ground, while the deeper players must learn to field the erratic kicks and advance upfield as best they can (Diagram 15-15).

You will encounter situations in which you are ahead late in the game and are receiving a kick-off. Since the onside kick is imminent, you want to align yourself as best you possibly can to field the ball (Diagram 15-16). We put ball handlers (quarterbacks, ends, running backs, defensive backs) at all eleven positions for this

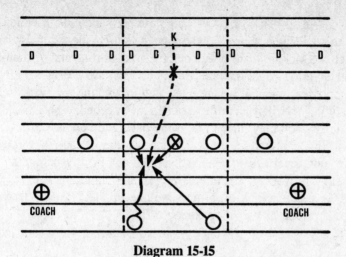

Diagram 15-15

Defending Inadvertent Short Kick or Surprise On-Side Kick

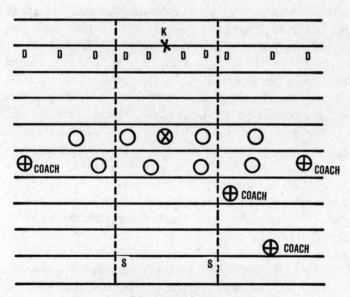

Diagram 15-16

"Hands" Team Receiving Short Kick-Off

"hands" team. There are two categories of situations in which you use this "Hands" team. In the first category, the setup is one in which the kicking team does not have enough time and/or time-outs to do anything to get the ball back once you have possession. In that case, possession is all we are interested in, and the receivers are told to ground the ball in *all* cases. In the second case, there is a possibility you may have to punt the ball to the opponent on fourth down. In that situation, we still coach the utmost caution, but we do allow our receivers to exercise judgement in advancing the ball upfield. We work on both kinds of "Hands" returns and every third time we practice kick-off returns we line up the "Hands" team and give them one or two short kicks to field.

GAME-TESTED PLACEMENT TEAM DRILLS

Since the goal posts were widened and the emphasis on place kicking has increased, both conversions and field goals have come to play a very large role in scholastic football. The kicker must have practice in working against the pressure of a rush. We introduce the place kick team to its duties at a midday session late in the first week of pre-season practice. We initially align the team against air and have the holder line up the tee, check to see if his team is set, then signal the center that he is ready. The center snaps the ball when ready, and the placement team steps into the blocking pattern. The one common rule for the place kick is that all protectors have the protection priority to the *inside*. There are various techniques for achieving this, but the inside must be protected. Since we do not have a starting count, we have a coach jump around on the defensive side to insure that we do not move before the snap as a result of such distractions by the defense (Diagram 15-17). We also put the ball down upfield on various hash locations and have the placement team dummy through several field goals. You must have your squad assume a coverage pattern after the ball is kicked (Diagram 15-18) and they must know the rules of the punting game since the placement is the same as a punt in terms of coverage and possession.

After the first placement practice, every alternate day in the pre-season we work two or three extra points live and one or two field goals live (Diagram 15-19). It is a good idea to use thirteen or

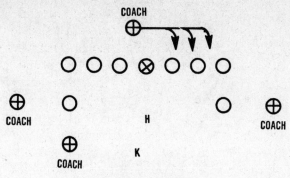

Diagram 15-17

Practicing Placements Versus Air

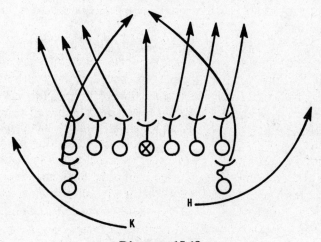

Diagram 15-18

Placement Coverage Versus Air

fourteen men to rush your placement man. If the theory and execution of your protection is correct, no amount of rushers will be able to block your attempts.

During the season, we take three or four extra points and one or two field goal attempts live once each week. We dummy several extra points and field goals on the day prior to the game. Note that we call the placement and break from the huddle so the squad is in

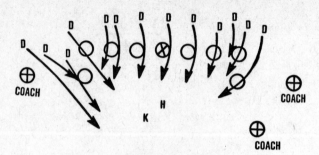

Diagram 15-19

Live Placement Drill

the habit of lining up on the ball from a huddle; this is a small point, but do not overlook it. Lining up offside or illegally shifting can cost you the game.

With the advent of the two point play, the fake placement should be a valuable weapon in high school and collegiate football. Just the fact that you have the play in your repertoire will soften the rush against your kicker. There are many possibilities for such plays, but we introduce ours with the placement team in the pre-season and practice them live once or twice in the pre-season, then we do it live once or twice the rest of the season. We dummy the plays every week before the game (Diagram 15-20).

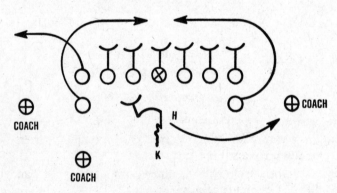

Diagram 15-20

Fake Placement Versus Air

GAME-TESTED DRILLS FOR DEFENSING THE PLACEMENT

You won't have to be in very many one- or two-point games to realize the importance of this phase of football. We work live in this drill every time we do it. We take our goal line defense and modify it in terms of techniques and personnel in order to work on a successful placement block scheme. Generally, the outside people attempt to penetrate and extend themselves over the kicking tee, while the inside people attempt to drive for penetration and get their hands up to block the kick. For that reason, tall players have an advantage on the interior of the placement rush, while quicker players are needed on the outside. We seldom practice the outside rush from both sides simultaneously, as we want to avoid collision injuries. A good placement defensive scheme also allows for coverage against fakes. Some defenders must be designated to remain back and defend the fake (Diagram 15-21).

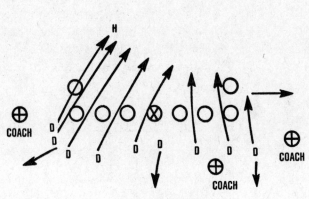

Diagram 15-21
Placement Defense Drill

We defend against the placements three times during the pre-season, throwing a couple of fakes in each time, and we defend against two placements each week during the season, occasionally working against a fake. If the scouting report shows that the team is likely to run the fake, we spend more time working on it. Also study your scouting report to ascertain whether the kicker is right- or left-footed, or if there are weaknesses in the snap or blocking, as you may want to adjust your scheme to allow for these differences.

It is also necessary to set up a return man for the long field goal attempt that you may have an opportunity to return. We only do this once or twice in the pre-season. We do it in the season in weeks when we face a particularly good long field goal kicker. Again, insure that your placement defense squad knows and understands the rules for scrimmage kicks. I saw a major collegiate game lost because the placement defense team did not know the rules.

If you want to elaborate, there are three distinct situations you may wish to prepare for in defending the placement. We have discussed the standard situation in which we are holding some people back to watch the fake. There are also situations in which you may want to commit an eleven-man rush without regard for the fake, or there is the case in which you want to minimize the rush and watch very carefully for the fake. You can adjust your regular scheme to provide for these contingencies and allow some practice time for them.

SIXTEEN

Covering the Field

SUBSTITUTION DRILLS

To use your personnel in the most efficient manner, it is necessary to assign special teams and substitution units for many of the different game situations that you may face. If you have been around high school players long, you know that they may forget to go in the game at the proper time unless they are well drilled in this procedure. We always post our depth charts for all special teams on the bulletin board on Monday so the players can see if any changes are effected. We practice almost all units during the week and the players who are expected to perform on each team have an opportunity to practice their assignments.

On the day prior to the game, we align primary and backup units for each special team on the field. Each unit is called from the bench and runs onto the field to align with the coaches (Diagram 16-1). A coach has 4″ x 6″ note cards with all special teams and backup units listed. When each unit lines up, he is particularly careful to check and make any adjustments necessary in case there has been an injury or change late in the week. We do this for offense, defense, punt, punt-return, kick-off, kick-off return, goal line defense, placement, placement defense, hands, and prevent teams. We only have a single unit for hands and prevent teams; there are two units assigned for all other phases.

After we insure that our personnel is set, we go to the sideline

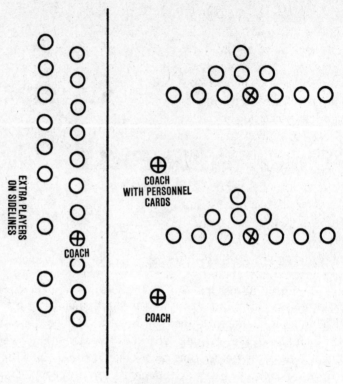

Diagram 16-1

Substitution Drill

and run the teams (primary units) on and off the field in the following order: (1) offense, (2) defense, (3) offense, (4) punt, (5) defense, (6) punt return, (7) offense, (8) placement, (9) kick-off, (10) defense, (11) goal line defense, (12) placement defense, (13) kick-off return, (14) offense, (15) prevent, and (16) hands. This sequence approximates most of the different situations in which they will substitute during the game. This drill is not physically demanding, but contributes to mental alertness that we want to emphasize on the day prior to the game.

SKULL PRACTICE AND TEAM/UNIT MEETINGS

We hold a team meeting prior to every practice and outline what we will teach during the practice. The meeting is held in the locker room with all the players dressed for practice and is limited to a maximum time of twenty minutes. The meeting is seldom that long and frequently is as short as five minutes. I do not believe in saturating a high school player with blackboard material after he has been sitting in a chair in a classroom all day. It is best to organize and prepare the material you are going to present on the blackboard so that you waste no time.

We sometimes hold quarterback meetings, defensive signal caller meetings, and assignment meetings after practice. A small classroom with a blackboard is best for this purpose. We have signal caller meetings once each week in the season and limit them to about fifteen minutes. We meet with signal callers several times during the pre-season after practice and limit the length of these sessions to fifteen minutes.

Assignments meetings are held with offensive centers, guards, tackles, ends, and defensive backs as separate groups. These meetings are held in the pre-season only once or twice, with a time limit of fifteen minutes. These are held after practice.

If you do not send in plays or defenses from the bench, you must spend quite a bit of time with your signal callers. Even if you call all the signals from the sideline, it is necessary to familarize the signal callers with the game plan; you can not execute any kind of play very well unless you have someone who is thoroughly conversant with all the whys and wherefores of your overall plan. Our procedure is to put different field positions on the blackboard and quiz our signal callers as to what to call for the different situations. We can add to field position other factors such as down and distance, time, weather conditions, opponent alignments, and so on.

SCOUT FILMS

Films of opponents have become an invaluable tool in game-by-game preparation. Along with the live scouting report, this source of research should provide good game preparation.

We break down opponent films as to formation and hash mark analyses, and prepare summaries just as we have described in previous chapters. We also thoroughly diagram the plays with the blocking assignments, as well as note all defenses for all situations, and report all elements of the kicking game. This is the basis of our game plan preparation in conjunction with what our team is capable of and in consideration of our live scouting reports.

We show our squad scout films on the day prior to the game. There was a time when we did this earlier in the week, but because of exigencies of time, we later decided to show the film on the day prior to the game, and it has worked well. At that stage of preparation, the physical work of practicing the game plan has been accomplished. The players should be acquainted with the team they are going to face and they should be mentally alert. Although your physical training has "tapered," the hay is not in the barn. A squad member can prepare mentally right up until game time. We think that watching the film at this time can crystallize the game plan and the mental preparation for a game that is only one day away. We do not show the film for a period of more than thirty minutes; we feel that a longer time period makes it difficult to maintain concentration.

GAME FILM CRITIQUE

We do not have an elaborate system of grading our players on their game performances. Instead, the head coach runs the projector while the players are seated near their position coaches who make corrections on techniques and assignments. It generally takes about one hour to critique a game film with the squad. The coaches spend some time and look at the film more thoroughly after the critique with the players, and may make any notes on something they especially want to recall, but again we do not grade the film. Personally, I think the best way to critique a game film is to have each position coach gather only his own group in the room when he critiques the film. We have tried this approach, but the problems of time and administration make it too difficult to implement on a regular basis.

THE INTRA-SQUAD SCRIMMAGE

We only do this twice a year. Other full-scale scrimmage is done against preparation squads. But in the pre-season we think it is a good idea to practice an all-out scrimmage with the best against the best. Our objectives for this scrimmage are: (1) the players should get a taste of full-scale game action against the best competition that we can provide from within the squad, (2) the coaching staff can evaluate personnel under full-scale conditions, and (3) progress can be determined for the squad in terms of offensive and defensive learning objectives.

We divide the number of plays we wish to run (in our case, 48-60) into four periods, so that:

1. In the first period, our first offense will scrimmage against the best defensive unit we can put together. If there are players who play both ways, they will play with the first offense in the period.

2. In the second period, our second offense will scrimmage against the best defensive personnel left. Some or many of these defenders may be first stringers on the offensive unit.

3. In the third period, our first defense will scrimmage against the best offense we can organize from the remaining available personnel.

4. In the fourth period, the second defense will scrimmage against the best offense we can put together from remaining personnel.

5. You can spot other substitutes in the scrimmage for certain situations or in cases of injuries. It is also advisable to have a fifth period and see that all remaining personnel get an opportunity to show their stuff. If the budget allows, it is a good idea to film and critique this scrimmage.

PRE-GAME AND HALFTIME WARM-UP

The purpose of the pre-game warm-up is to: (1) prepare the player to compete on a physiological basis, (2) to get a minimal amount of practice with some fundamentals, so the players are fine-tuned for the game, (3) to shake out some of the pre-game nervousness, and (4) to prepare for specific field and weather conditions. We have the specialists take the field eight minutes before the rest of the squad. The backs work with and against the wind. Placement people take no more than a dozen kicks which include extra points, field goals from various positions, and kick-offs. Punters take the same number of punts, angling a couple for the coffin corner. Safeties, placement holders, and long snappers also work during this period.

When the full squad is on the field, we take our preliminary stretching in the same manner we do before practice except the entire team is led by the co-captains. After the stretching, linemen are drilled by the line coaches. They go through the same procedure as for everyday offensive line drills except they do not use shields. The defenders are semi-live and offer some resistance. After that is concluded, the ends go to a group with the backs to catch some passes, and the rest of the offensive line goes through a pass protection drill, again with the defenders semi-live (Diagram 16-2). The offensive line then goes through an assignment drill and discussion of any assignment adjustments, etc. (Diagram 16-3).

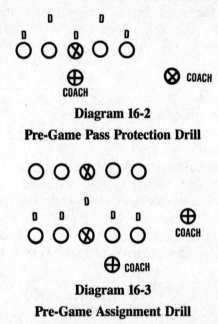

Diagram 16-2

Pre-Game Pass Protection Drill

Diagram 16-3

Pre-Game Assignment Drill

Backs take their preliminary starts as in everyday offensive drills, then line up in two lines and simply catch softly thrown passes from the quarterbacks. When they are joined by the ends, wingbacks and ends make sharp pass breaks and the quarterbacks zing the ball to them while the other backs still catch the soft passes. After about six to eight minutes of catching passes, the backs and line come together and run a signal drill with as many offensive teams as we can put together. It gives us some team starts and good ball handling work. We call the plays from the line of scrimmage and run against air. A trip halfway up the field and back is usually all we want. We then return to the dressing room.

When we come out for the game, the players stretch and take a few starts on their own. The quarterbacks throw a few passes to each other to get warm again.

When we come out for the second half, we encourage the players to stretch and take a few starts on their own. We then organize them and have them run about five or six plays for a signal drill, in which we accomplish the same objectives as before the game. This team warm-up for the second half is something we have done for about five years. We feel that running the signal drill has improved us in comparison to a period of years when we would come out and look rather sluggish at the beginning of the second half.

INDIVIDUAL TAKE-HOME DRILLS

If you do not conduct an organized summer program or if your players cannot get to team workouts in the off-season, it is important to give them guidelines to get themselves ready to play. We want to see the players in good enough physical condition so that fatigue does not impede their progress in pre-season drills. We want them to improve their strength, sprint speed, flexibility, and agility. We also want the player to develop his individual specialty techniques such as kicking, passing, centering, and so on.

The standard program that we ask the players to do begins with our conventional stretching that we do before every practice. We add to this routine: (1) an exercise in which the player stretches out with his back against a wall and to get as much of his back surface against the wall as possible, with the arms straight and overhead and against the wall. After six seconds of good stretching that way, (2) we have the player sit down with toes up and legs on the floor, back and hips against the wall, arms extended straight up. Again we want as much back surface as possible to contact the wall or the floor. (3) We have the player stand up, take a couple of steps out from the wall and bend over backwards, then put his hands on the wall and "walk" down and back up the wall. (4) We ask the player to turn around and put both hands on the wall and kick as high as possible to the side with the right foot. The knee is relaxed and the player concentrates the weight of his leg in his big toe. He takes twenty of these wall kicks with the right foot and then repeats the procedure with his left foot. (5) We then have the player do a hurdler's spread, sitting on the ground with one leg doubled and out to the side, the other leg straight out in front so that the two legs form a right angle. The extended leg should be flat on the ground with the knee down and the toes pointing directly to the sky. The player takes ten smooth reaches with his head and attempts to touch the knee with the nose. It is imperative to keep the knee down; in time, most players will probably be able to reach the knee or extend even further.

We ask the players to do starts just as we do in every day offensive drills in practice, then run two 40-yard dashes as fast as possible. We ask them to do the same agility drills that we have the defensive ends do.

We ask the players to follow the weightlifting routine that we establish for them during the football season. We want them to lift three times each week, never on consecutive days.

We give the players a series of form running drills that we feel will improve their running style:

1. The first form running drill is the high knee drill in which they are asked to run forty yards by taking eighty steps, getting the knees as high as possible, pointing the toes straight ahead, pumping the arms with the elbows close to the side. We assign two repetitions of that drill.

2. We also have the players do the "drum-major," which is a long stride pointing the toes with good arm action, except that the runner is leaning back, as a drum major would. That is also a two repetition exercise, each time for a distance of forty yards.

3. We have each player overstride forty yards for two repetitions. Each repetition consists of taking off from the ball of one foot, landing on the ball of the other foot, then extending again. The object is for each player to count his strides for each repetition and see how much he improves over the summer. If he can increase his natural stride only one inch, he has gained considerable speed.

All specialists are given written copies of individual drills that we have previously outlined. They are expected to gain skill in their techniques over the summer.

Index